EIGHTY YEARS

OF

REPUBLICAN GOVERNMENT

IN

THE UNITED STATES.

EIGHTY YEARS

OF

REPUBLICAN GOVERNMENT

IN

THE UNITED STATES.

BY LOUIS J. JENNINGS.

FIRST AMERICAN FROM THE SECOND LONDON EDITION

NEW YORK:
CHARLES SCRIBNER & CO.,
1868.

Published by arrangement with the Author.

PREFACE.

THE object of the following pages is to explain the original plan and design of the American Constitution, to review the changes which have been made in it in subsequent times, and to describe its present condition and mode of working.

To fulfil these ends the author has examined with care the writings and speeches of the eminent men who framed the great fundamental law of the United States. In their declared opinions, and in the debates which took place in the State Conventions upon the ratification of the Constitution, can alone be found a true embodiment of the aims and ideas of the community which established the Republic. In the author's attempt to portray the government as it is, he has pursued a similar method of investigation;—that is, he has founded his statements and based his conclusions upon authority which ought to be accepted in England, because no one challenges it in America. For two years past — probably the most important two years in the history of the United States government, if we consider all the changes they have brought to pass—the author's daily duties called him into close intercourse with many of the most active public men of the country. He had great opportunities afforded him for acquiring the information he sought, for, although it is often said that Americans will never willingly expose themselves to criticism, the writer of these pages never detected any evidence of that disposition. The Americans do not take offence at a candid and fair discussion of the government under which they live. They are not well pleased to be caricatured; but they are not the only people in the world who object to be represented abroad by travesties of their political and social life.

In the work here placed before the reader the author has occupied himself with facts, and his authorities may be found cited at the foot of the page. He has had no favourite theory which he wished to enforce by the example of America. He has simply endeavoured to ascertain what the government of the United States was intended to be, and how far it has departed from the first design. He has not desired to prove that Democracy or Republicanism must necessarily be a success, or necessarily a failure, or that it is better or worse than other systems of government, or that it is anything more than a form of polity still open to diligent study and investigation. Apart from and theories whatever, he has traced the results of eighty years of Republican Government; and if it can be proved that he is in error upon any question here discussed, his regret will be lessened by the knowledge that he errs in company with some of the greatest Americans that have adorned the public life or literature of their country.

LONDON, *November*, 1867.

CONTENTS.

CHAPTER I.

CHAPTER II.

CHAPTER III.

CHAPTER IV.

CHAPTER V.

CHAPTER VI.

CHAPTER VII.

CHAPTER VIII.

CHAPTER IX.

CHAPTER X.

CHAPTER XI.

CHAPTER XII.

ALPHABETICAL TABLE OF CONTENTS.

EIGHTY YEARS

OF

REPUBLICAN GOVERNMENT.

CHAPTER I.

THE THEORY OF THE GOVERNMENT.

THE political system of the United States is based upon the theory that the people have an indefeasible right to choose their own form of government, and to modify or change it whenever a sufficiently large proportion agree that change is necessary. They endured all the hardships and losses incidental to a revolution in order to rid themselves of monarchical government and a hereditary ruler; any rule claiming to bear prescriptive rights they were determined never to have again. They resolved to govern for themselves. A qualified share of political power is committed to the people in constitutional Europe avowedly as a trust; in the American Republic the supreme power is exercised by the people as a right. The original Constitution was an instrument prepared with the object of carrying into effect the wishes and opinions of a community of thirteen States, and it remains in force only during the pleasure of the nation which has since risen up. The Constitution itself recommitted the power which it assumed back to the people, its original depositaries, when it prescribed the means by which amendments could in after times be made. The voice of the people is the supreme law. They elect their agents and representatives; and while each of these agents may be held to a strict account for his actions, while the most solemn proceedings of the Legislative may be annulled by the Judiciary,[1] and the Executive be controlled by the Legislative, the acts of the people alone are above all judgment or review. They are not restrained by precedents; in a government depending upon popular will there can be no law of precedent. The people create a precedent or destroy one as circumstances seem to require. "No man," said Mr. Webster, "makes a question that the people are the source of all political power. Government is constituted for their good, and its members are their ministers and servants. He who would argue against this must argue without an adversary. The aggregate community, the collected will of the people, is sovereign."[2] Be the faults or errors of the government what they may, the people alone are

---

[1] This is the *theory* of the Constitution. Whether the Judiciary could sustain its decision or not, is another question.

[2] Argument in the Rhode Island case, 27th Jan. 1848. Webster's Works, vol. vi., p. 221.

responsible for their existence. The idle, the improvident, the unsuccessful cannot, as is too readily done in other countries, cast the blame of their misfortunes or sufferings upon the government. Everett, who represented New England opinion more accurately than any other one man, congratulated his countrymen upon the perfection of their government as exhibited in the fact that "no measure of policy, public or private, domestic or foreign, could long be pursued against the will of a majority of the people." The system is one which professes to guard with more than paternal care the welfare and interests of every class of the community. It lays claim to the credit of giving more liberty and diffusing greater happiness than any other form of government, and the mass of the people fully believe that it claims no more than it is entitled to. A contemporary American writer boasts that in the United States the best hopes of man may find their accomplishment; that there is neither failure nor disappointment in the government; that under it a perfect commonwealth might become a reality.[3] If there had not been a large majority who felt this to be the truth, the Union would have perished long ago. What, then, are the principles of this "perfect commonwealth?" Is it true that owing to its superior wisdom the masses of the people are better represented and protected than they are anywhere else in the world? Is it indeed

---

[3] 'North American Review,' Oct. 1865, art. VIII.

a government fit to stand as an everlasting model for the guidance of mankind? If it be this, it is of vital consequence to the whole human race that its merits should be rightly understood; and if there be defects in it, great and mischievous defects, the same consideration demands that they should be openly stated and discussed.

The government of the United States is divided into three departments—the Executive, the Legislative, and the Judiciary. The appointment of the Federal Judicial Officers rests with the President, subject to the approval of the Senate; the Senate is chosen by the local Legislature of each State, which in its turn is elected by the people; and thus, although the people are the primary source of power, they have only a broken and indirect influence in the selection of the Judiciary. In most of the States the judges are elected by universal suffrage, but this pernicious custom has not yet extended to the organization of the highest legal tribunal of the Republic.

For the Executive the people vote through the agency of electors whom they choose at the polls. For members of the House of Representatives they vote without the intervention of other agents. In the government of each State the inhabitants exercise control which is not broken by artificial checks, or conducted through side channels, as is the case with respect to the higher Federal offices. The laws of the State are settled by the local Legislature, which as a rule meets once a year, and the members of which are regularly elected by popular vote. Once in a certain term, which varies in different States, the people have the opportunity of calling a Convention to revise the State laws, and to this Convention they can send representatives who will carry out the desired reform. The frequency of elections, which De Tocqueville considers so great an evil, is nevertheless a material part of the mechanism of government in America, and it was greatly relied upon by the framers of the Constitution as one great source of stability in the new system. By this means the wishes and wants of the people are continually being made known. There can be no hidden grievances, no discontents to ferment unseen and imperil the Republic. Once in every two years the people may completely change the popular branch of the Legislature. If Congress opposes itself to their desires and opinions, its action may be checked by the judgment of the people before its term has expired.[4] The President holds office for four years, but he is not beyond the reach of the people during that period. They may return a House of Representatives which is adverse to him, and gradually pursue the same course with the Senate, through their local Legislatures, until he can no longer use his veto

[4] Each Congress sits for three sessions (formerly two), which extend over two years. The elections for the ensuing Congress take place, in the majority of States, five or six months before the one actually sitting has fulfilled its term.

power with any effect, and he is thus rendered subordinate to the Legislative. Years may pass during which the nation is content to let its affairs be managed by its rulers as they may see fit; but the moment it is seriously dissatisfied, the moment its confidence is broken or a danger seems to menace the country, from that moment it can begin to recall its delegated power, and practically order its policy at home and abroad. It is only a qualified trust which the people yield to their representatives. They are themselves politicians by habit and custom. Every other year they are called upon to decide what principles they wish advanced, and which men they desire to advocate them.

Whether a government of this nature is the one above all others most advantageous to society is a question open to much dispute, but that an essential requisite of good government is practicable under the system—namely, that it shall be strong and efficient, and capable of maintaining its place among nations—it is impossible to deny. That of the United States passed through the tremendous assaults made upon it in the civil war with resolution and success which could not have been excelled had it been in the hands of a small and privileged class. It gained in security by submitting itself wholly to the guidance of the majority. It was the servant of the people, and the people came forward as one man to its support. They prized it, and by their instrumentality it was saved from destruction when a section of the country became dissatisfied, and sought to form itself into a distinct nation. Burden after burden was laid upon them, sacrifice after sacrifice demanded, and instead of complaining they came again and again, demanding greater burdens and offering greater sacrifices, and continued to display the same lavish spirit long after the war was over. Popular government saved the Union in 1861, and the government of a privileged class could have done no more.

But in such periods as these we behold the government in its most attractive aspect. The patriotism and spirit of the people are evoked, a power unsuspected even by themselves is made manifest to the world, and in the splendour and renown of victory all defects and shortcomings are overlooked. We see everything through a false and exaggerated medium. From a disbelief in the country, the public mind goes over with unthinking and infatuated eagerness to the worship of all its institutions. Nothing, it is argued, can be amiss in a form of policy which survived the shocks of 1861-65, and came out of the trial apparently strong enough to pass through another equally severe. But if the old prejudices against the American Union were mischievous and unreasonable, this attachment to it without a cause is likely to produce still more evil consequences. No American of eminence has ever yet denied the existence of great and peculiar failings in his government. That these imperfections should now be questioned or lost sight of by the rest of the world is greatly owing to a reaction in the public feeling produced by the failure of the prophecies relative to the fall of the Union. Many writers have predicted the inevitable collapse of American democracy directly it was opposed to its first searching test, reasoning very often upon imaginary parallels in the history of other nations, and forgetting that the experiment is being tried in the United States under circumstances so exceptional as to put to confusion all speculative or philosophical theories upon systems of government. The exceedingly favourable conditions under which the people live, although habitually acknowledged in general terms, are seldom properly appreciated. It is indeed hard to realise them fully. Setting aside altogether the physical advantages enjoyed by the Americans, due consideration has not been given to the fact that in the majority is vested the power to amend the government whenever it falls short of their necessities. The Constitution by which a small community was originally governed, and which sufficed for that period, is not to be regarded as an instrument destined to place a limit upon thought, progress, and improvement. It is not a band of iron which is to hold the nation in a fixed position for ever. Not the Constitution, but the popular will, is what gives government its powers in America. A written Constitution cannot retard or hinder the growth of principles, least of all in an active and young community, full of nervous energy, and quickness, and eager life. Where the people create the government they will be above the government. The American, as one of their own writers justly remarks, "never loses sight of the fact that government is only a device founded on expediency; and he keeps in mind that it possesses no intrinsic right to exist, and that it is always subject to the arbitration of the popular right of revolution."[5] A government which had its birth in revolution, and that in quite recent times, cannot be considered master of the people. They will not look upon its first inception as a Divine inspiration with which it would be sacrilege to meddle. It must expand with their growth, and be treated as the work of men like unto themselves, while its fundamental principles, so far as they are consistent with liberty and justice, are scrupulously preserved. But if the Constitution is to retain the authority ascribed to it by all American jurists, as "a code of positive law,"[6] binding upon all persons and upon all departments of the government, it should be altered and amended only by the means dictated in the instrument itself. If one part of the nation, having temporary command of the national armies, alters and adapts it to its own purposes without consulting the other part, what becomes of it as a code of positive law? It then changes with the fortunes of every party, perhaps with every election. The form of government is, in truth, of little importance to

---

[5] 'North American Review,' Oct. 1865.

[6] This phrase is used by Mr. R. H. Dana, junr., in his very valuable notes to 'Wheaton,' p. 54.

America so far as its present prosperity is concerned. Call the nominal ruler king, emperor, or president, and the material interests of the people must still flourish while land is plentiful, while the country is covered with small proprietors, while labour is scarce and wages high. These conditions not unnaturally sometimes lead the people themselves to attribute to a political system the blessings which they really owe to nature. In a land of universal prosperity men do not find fault with the government under which they live. It has been said that in the number of small landed proprietors consists the true strength of a nation. Undoubtedly it is a source of strength to the American Union. Abstract arguments against democracy prove nothing against the American government, because it is a democracy existing under conditions which would make any method of government successful. Democracy there, it is sometimes asserted, must fail because democracy from its very nature cannot be enduring, and it is also assumed, and so far as we can at present judge with entire truth, that the American people never would consent to adopt any other form of government. Thus the philosophers end by leaving the Americans without a government of any kind. They hand them over to a reign of anarchy. It is true that the evidence of facts is wholly opposed to such reasonings. What we find in the United States is that the people possess a government which they have the power of adapting to their ends, although not in the manner theoretically assigned, as we shall presently see, and one with which the majority of the people are content, because it is always in the power of the majority to do as they please with it. Whether the Americans as a *nation* will always remain content is a question concerning which very grave doubts may be entertained, but they have at least as much reason on their side in believing, from their past history, that their government is indestructible, as other nations have in predicting its sudden downfall. There will always be a large, probably a preponderating, party ready to fight for the maintenance of the Union.

There is another circumstance which in the United States lessens the ordinary risk of intrusting the controlling influence in the government to the masses. There the people are accustomed to the duties, although it would be too much to say that they are always mindful of the responsibilities, of government. If they have not explored all the byeways of political philosophy, they are used to the practical management of their own affairs. They may know little of political science, but they are generally shrewd men of business. Each State makes its own laws, and hence it is that the laws of all the States differ in material respects. The United States Supreme Court has no jurisdiction over them, except when they involve some question or privilege the treatment of which is definitively prescribed by the Constitution. Laws relating to property, marriage, education, the punishment of crime, the preservation of social order, the entire regulation of the affairs of a community, are made by the States for themselves, with the one qualification that they must not be in conflict with the Constitution. And who are the law-makers? The delegates elected by the people—and they are no more than delegates. They constantly consult the sense and wishes of their constituents; and if they frame an obnoxious law, another set of representatives are sent to the State Legislatures the following year to repeal it. It might almost be said that the people are every day of their lives engaged in practising the active duties of government. The Federal Legislature is only in plan the State Legislature on a larger scale. It is an expansion of the local principle of self-government.

In America, then, as the people make their government, and know that they are responsible for it, they submit willingly to its decrees. Lord Brougham thought it a special merit of the English government that it could levy taxes, in case of need, more quietly and successfully than any other. "If it be said," he continued, "that the American government can as well call forth the resources of the people, I have very grave doubt if the national representatives, and especially the President towards the end of his first three years, would inflict a heavy excise or a grinding income-tax upon the people, as our Parliament has so often done; and I have no doubt at all that such an infliction would very speedily lead to a termination of hostilities without any very great nicety about the terms of peace."[7] The signal manner in which this confident prediction has been falsified can never be forgotten, any more than the prediction itself can be repeated. Not only did the American people submit to unparalleled income and excise taxes, and every other kind of tax, during the civil war, but they afterwards accepted these enormous imposts quite voluntarily, paid them almost without a murmur from one end of the country to the other, and continue to pay them to this hour. Could any people do more for their government than this? And why do the Americans make these sacrifices? Because they are deeply, immoveably attached to a certain national ideal, which some believe has been realized already, and others hope to see realized in the future; because they feel that there is no part of their government in which they have not an influence and an interest; because they believe that it exists for their benefit and welfare, and that when it ceases to do so they can rapidly amend or remodel it.

These vital reforms are expedient and justifiable as often as they are necessary. Washington, in his farewell address, emphatically said to the people, "the basis of our political systems is the right of the people to make and to alter their constitutions of government." Judge Story remarks of the Constitu-

---

7 Lord Brougham on the 'British Constitution,' chapter xvii.

tion that "its framers were not bold or rash enough to believe or to pronounce it to be perfect. They made use of the best lights which they possessed to form and adjust its parts, and mould its materials. But they knew that time might develop many defects in its arrangements, and many deficiencies in its powers. They desired that it might be open to improvement, and, under the guidance of the sober judgment and enlightened skill of the country, to be perpetually approaching nearer and nearer to perfection."[8] Upon these principles the American people determined that the country should be governed after the great rebellion. There were not wanting those who contended that the Constitution was binding upon the nation for ever, and could neither be abridged nor extended, no matter what perils or difficulties arose. A decision of five judges of the Supreme Court[9] in the case of a man named Milligan, who had been imprisoned under the order of a military commission, and who petitioned for release, gave authority and sanction to this party. The judges went so far as to say of the Constitution that "no doctrine involving more pernicious consequences was ever invented by the wit of man than that any of its provisions can be suspended during any of the great emergencies of the government." But the Chief Justice and three other judges dissented from this opinion, and held that Congress, in times of

[8] 'Commentaries,' § 417 (3rd edition, Boston, 1858).

[9] Delivered at the December term, 1866.

extraordinary emergency, had the right to put in force extraordinary powers for the preservation of the country. And common sense confirms this interpretation of the law. If, of the Union or the Constitution one or other must fall, which is it for the interest of the people to abandon? Had the Southern States conquered, Union and Constitution would both have perished. The Northern people fought to save both, but a strict adherence to the Constitution was found during the struggle to be inconsistent with the preservation of the Union, and it was therefore practically disregarded. At first, indeed, it was only sought to alter it in accordance with the terms of constitutional law, that is by the consent of a majority of three-fourths of *all* the States; but since the Southern States would not voluntarily sign away their liberty, this provision was ignored, and the decision of the conquering States was held to be alone sufficient to recast the agreement of 1787.

The light in which the Americans regard their government can never be understood unless we suppose it to have a double existence—an existence in fact and an existence in the imagination or hopes of the people. The foreign observer describes only what he sees; the American invests his government with certain fictitious qualities which he knows that it ought to possess, and would possess if the ideas of its founders were truly carried out, and which he retains a firm belief will be grafted upon it by the good sense of his posterity. You show the American the errors of his government in practice, and he replies by drawing a vivid picture of it as it presents itself to his fancy. It is not always easy in an inquiry upon American affairs to distinguish between the real and the ideal. If the wishes of those who made the Constitution, and the desires of the educated class, could prevail, there would be a perfect government in the United States, and the American will sometimes assert that such a privilege does belong to him. But when its faults and its errors are pointed out he at once changes his ground, and pleads that the country is new, that it has already achieved wonders in a short time, and that there is every reason to suppose it will continue to improve and progress. These arguments are entitled to the utmost attention and respect, but if the admissions which they contain were more carefully borne in mind there would be no necessity to urge them. So much would not be looked for in the American government, because no extravagant pretensions would be made by those who undertake to defend it against criticism. But when Americans challenge comparison with the rest of the world, it is only a proper tribute to them to examine into their claims. They ought to wish all their fellow-creatures the enjoyment of the same blessings which they possess, but in order to induce the world to avail itself of them it must first be taught to appreciate the boon. This cannot be done without explanation and inquiry. Foreign criticisms may often be full of fallacies, but these fallacies as frequently give the American system praise which it does not deserve as they detract from its just merits. The favourite ideal of the Americans, though doubtless exceedingly noble and attractive in itself, is probably still further from conveying a true idea of the government as it is. What that ideal is we shall have an opportunity of ascertaining in a subsequent chapter, and the proof will be given from American history and American writers that it differs widely from the state of things which actually exists. Nothing was more essential to the original theory of the government than that there should be one great law by which all questions affecting the interests of different sections of the country should be judged and decided, and yet that law is now mainly a thing of the past. Again, what was so much sought after by the early statesmen, or what was so precious to the people, as the maintenance of State independence? It was the very life-blood of the system. But time and events have transformed the government, without bringing it any nearer to the ideal of the people. Now, as immediately after the war of independence, they are willing to sacrifice almost everything for the sake of securing an irresistible power at some central point. Any one who wishes to describe the working of the American government must study, not the Constitution of 1787, but the records of parties, the acts of the Legislature, the events of the last five-and-twenty years, and the history of the country as it is written upon the statute-books. The Constitution shows what the government was intended to be, and in so far as it does this it is still valuable. Contemporary history and legislation alone show what the government really is. The Constitution has not been expressly abandoned, for the homage of the lips is still paid to it. But it has been subjected to so many violent changes that its framers, could they see it once more, would detect but few traces of their work. Yet one doctrine of the former government is still preserved—namely, that all power belongs to the people. Before that doctrine is accepted as the wisest yet discovered in the science of governing mankind it would be well to see what is the effect of its practical application in the United States. But in times of popular agitation reason, facts, and arguments are no more than straws before the wind, and the examples and warnings presented by the American government are misconstrued or disregarded.

CHAPTER II.

THE STATE AND THE UNION.

THE authors of the Constitution proposed to themselves an undertaking which no human ingenuity could have accomplished. Thirteen States which had been accustomed to make their own laws, to decide what taxes they should pay, and generally to control their own affairs, were to be brought together by a common bond. It was to be a bond strong enough to render a general government practicable, and yet not so strong as to impair the efficiency or independence of the local governments. It was to be elastic enough to enclose new members of the Federation, and its pressure was to be equally distributed over all parts. It was to endure for all ages, and be capable of satisfying the requirements of as many millions as there were thousands in the Confederacy. A complex machine was set in motion, constructed by many hands, and with pieces inserted in various points at the last moment to gratify caprice or appease jealousies. There were independent parts in it which always had a tendency to come into collision, and which yet were supposed to be certain to go on working independently for ever. Small local ambitions and great national aspirations were alike to be satisfied. The community might progress, new interests might arise, new conditions of life be forced upon the people. But the general theory of the government, it was thought, could never need reconstruction. It was imperishable, perfect in all its parts, secure in all its details, destined to be the wonder and envy of the world as at once the most just and most beneficent form of government which a nation of free men ever had the wisdom to choose for themselves.

A very few years elapsed before there began to be discovered in this carefully studied plan many unfortunate deficiencies. The newly created power threatened to swallow up the old one. The States were always in alarm for the preservation of their rights. The Federal government was regarded with affection because it was believed to confer many inestimable benefits upon the people. It was in purpose a just and fair government; it left every man free to enjoy the fruits of his labour, unless he were a slave; and it relieved the public mind from the fear of foreign aggression. But there were critical misunderstandings in the community, and very early in the history of the new commonwealth they seemed likely to produce disastrous consequences. The very soldiers who had fought together against the English regiments quarrelled bitterly on questions relating to their several States. "The Southern troops," wrote Washington's adjutant general, "comprising the regiments south of the Delaware, looked with very unkind feelings on those of New England." And Washington himself was obliged to rebuke in general orders the "jealousies" which had "arisen among the troops from the different provinces," and more than once he betrayed in his private letters the uneasiness which these bickerings caused him.[1] The vote upon the adoption of the Constitution, even after a number of amendments had been made to it, stood 187 in its favour and 168 against—and thus by a majority of nineteen only was it held to be binding upon the States. The dissatisfaction of this very powerful minority, and the early internal dissensions, grew more alarming every year.[2] In 1792 Jefferson advised Washington to serve as President a second term, in order that he might guard against "violence and secession." In a few years there rapidly sprung up a series of disputes upon questions of commerce, upon slavery, upon protection, upon tariff laws.[3] The discussion whether States had or had not a right to withdraw from the Union without molestation runs through the whole history of the country down to the time when the great issue was decided on the battle-fields of the South. Slavery was only the most important of a

---

[1] Sparkes' 'Life of Washington,' and Fowler's 'Sectional Controversy' (New York, 1865), p. 12.

[2] Story's 'Commentaries' (3rd ed.), book iii. chap. ii.

[3] Fowler's 'Sectional Controversy,' pp. 12, 41, 52, 66, 108, 110, 133.

number of circumstances which had a tendency to dissolve the Union. Almost every State that has ever felt itself aggrieved threatened to quit the Federation. Massachusetts has done so repeatedly. During the war of 1812 there occurred an angry contention with respect to the authority of the central government over the militia of the States. On one side it was affirmed that the government could call out the militia when it pleased; on the other it was insisted that the States alone possessed this right. The governor of Massachusetts was one of the many men in office who took the popular view, and maintained that the powers of the Federal government were limited by the Constitution, and that the State legislatures were "the guardians, not only of individuals, but of the sovereignty of their respective States." A representative in Congress from Massachusetts said that the Federal government could not claim any power by implication, but that the State governments might. The press and the pulpit of New England insisted energetically on their right of separation, and many years afterwards Mr. Webster, in the course of his celebrated discussion with Hayne in the Senate, said—"We, sir, who oppose the Carolina doctrine do not deny that the people may, if they choose, throw off any government when it becomes oppressive and intolerable, and erect a better in its stead." It is useless to multiply these illustrations. The doctrine that the States were left free to choose whether they would remain in the

Union or detach themselves from it, was never refuted, though it was occasionally contradicted, until the Southern States unwisely precipitated the decision in 1861.

It was not possible that a good understanding could be preserved between the Federal power and the governments of the States by a written Constitution. On the contrary, such a compact was likely to deepen old animosities, and inflame local jealousies. It was only by the studied employment in the Constitution of vague and disputable terms that the assent of the majority of the States was procured. The demands which could not be satisfied were evaded. The language in which the instrument was drawn up left each side free to suppose that it had gained the victory. The advocates of the central government, and the advocates of State rights, either considered that they had triumphed, or that all the questions between them were still left open. This intentional ambiguity was only cleared away by a civil war more angry and bloody, and entailing greater miseries upon the conquered, than any other recorded in history. If the Constitution had been what some believed, and all hoped it was, it would have prevented this contest. However difficult it might have been in 1787 to put sectional disagreements at rest, it would have cost the people less then to have attempted the task than it cost them in 1861. The leaves of the Sibyl had eventually to be purchased at a fearful price, and the secret written upon them was found to be—"absolute submission to the majority, indissolubility of the Union." The "sovereignty" and "independence" of the States are henceforth hemmed in within positive limits by the sword and the bayonet. A State which enters the Union can never leave it again. The first parties to the contract might have pleaded that they misread it and were deceived, but those who accept it now do so with their eyes fully open to its obligations and the penalty of infringing them. Had it been so explicit at first there would have been no war of secession, because there would have been no Union. The States in 1787-89 would never have signed away their independent powers. They held certain principles which, so far from being odious, no one attempted to controvert. Less than eighty years afterwards the practical application of those same principles ruined eleven millions of people, annihilated their commerce, deprived them of all political or social rights, and laid their property and their persons at the mercy of their conquerors. The Constitution itself was the primary cause of these calamities. It did not expressly forbid secession; it did not expressly countenance it. It was quite possible for conscientious men, North and South, sincerely to believe they were in the right. The Constitution was purposely framed so that it might be read in two ways. The North chose one reading, the South the other, and thus it befell that the sins of the fathers were visited upon the children, and the South bore the penalty which is exacted when one generation shifts its duties and responsibilities to another.

Under the influence of an organic national law which every side might interpret as it pleased, which might be held to mean one thing one week and a totally different thing the next, the whole character of the government has been changed. No one can now say with any certainty what will be even its chief features in ten years to come. The alluring ambition to become a great nation, respected if possible, but certainly feared, by the rest of the world, is displacing the early attachment to the independence of States. At first the Union was designed to be a Federation, with sufficient powers at the central point to preserve it from outer attack, and to secure a just performance of the obligations which had been entered into by the contracting States. The evils suffered under the old Confederation had proyed to the people the necessity of a strong government, and they wished to construct a government as strong as was consistent with the rights of States. There was nothing so dear to the people as the integrity of their local systems. The Federal government was intended to be an amplification of the State government. Each State has its Legislature, which is divided into two Houses, and there is an Executive at the head who, as often as the Legislature meets—generally once a year—prepares a message describing the condition and necessities of the community. The two Houses then proceed to adjust the finances of the State, and pass such laws as are deemed expedient. In all these details a close parallel can be perceived in the Federal government. Could it be supposed that these two powers, the greater and the lesser, would constantly work side by side together in harmony?

The conflict was indeed unavoidable. The ambition of the Federal Legislature was certain to increase, and it was left by the Constitution to run its course without restraint. The Executive was armed only with a qualified veto, which, when party passions ran high, might easily be rendered completely unavailing. The Judiciary could not interpose until it was too late to undo anything. It had no initiatory action, and if its decision gave offence it was doubtful whether it could save even itself for long together. We should depreciate the sagacity of the founders of the Constitution if we supposed that they were unconscious of these elements of discord. But they trusted to the future to discover safeguards and remedies which they did not dare to propose. They looked upon their work when it was finished with quite as much disquietude as admiration. "Hamilton, Washington, and others," says an American writer, "regarded democracy as a very doubtful experiment. They made the Constitution as conservative as they dared to make it, but they knew well it was a fragile bark, freighted with a precious cargo, and launched on the waves of a treacherous and tempestuous sea. They looked in vain for the elements that give strength and endurance to the British government, the church, the aristocracy, the throne, each connected with the past and the future, each presenting bulwarks like rocks to the surges of popular passion."[4] They would have been affrighted at the bare vision of universal suffrage and the supremacy of a democracy, stripped of all the "checks and balances" which they vainly imagined would be everlasting, levelling all distinctions of intellect or station throughout the land. But anarchy was behind them, and they were obliged to go forward into darkness and doubt. They bequeathed the dangers from which they shrank to their descendants, and it was an inheritance of evil which went on accumulating until it deluged the land with blood.

It has been said that a powerful central government was the boon which men like Washington and Madison sought to give the people. In the Federal Convention which drew up the draft of the Constitution, and in the State Conventions which afterwards ratified it, the same idea was constantly expressed.[5] The old Confederation had led to great injustices. Connecticut complained, for instance, that, while it had borne a heavy share of the burden caused by the war, other States refused to pay anything.[6] The

---

4 Fisher's 'Trial of the Constitution,' p. 71. See also chapter xii., on the 'Prospects of the Union.'

5 Elliot's 'Debates' in the Constitutional Conventions, ii. pp. 102-3, 196, &c.

6 See also a speech made by Mr. Hamilton in the Convention of New York, Elliot's 'Debates,' ii. p. 232.

Confederation was abandoned expressly because of the absence in it of a central power. In the Convention of 1787 Mr. Randolph urged that a mere Federation of the States would not be sufficient, and he moved a resolution that "a national government ought to be established consisting of a supreme, legislative, and judiciary."[7] This was carried by a vote of six against one. There were others in the Convention who would have circumscribed the authority of the States, if they had dared, once for all, but the temper of the people forbade the attempt. Then they thought it better to possess an appreciable share in the government of a "sovereign State" than to be units in a nation. The belief of the "Fathers" was that the federal system would always be, by its very organization, dependent upon the State system. To use the figure which is in every child's mouth in America, the central government was the sun, and the State governments the planets which revolved round it. "The Union," said Hamilton when the subject was being discussed in the Convention of New York, "is dependent on the will of State governments for its chief magistrate and for its Senate. The blow aimed at the members must give a fatal wound to the head, and the destruction of the States must be at once a political suicide."[8] The State governments can never be invaded, was the cry with which Madison and his colleagues were constantly obliged to allay the distrust of the people. They

[7] Madison's 'Reports,' p. 132. [8] Elliot's 'Debates,' ii. p. 353.

were met with such answers as the following:—"It appears to me that the State governments are not sufficiently secured, and that they may be swallowed up by the great mass of powers given to Congress. State governments are the basis of our happiness, security, and prosperity."[9] The very phrase "We the people" provoked a storm of objections in several of the Conventions, because it seemed to imply a consolidation of all the States. "Will any gentleman say," asked a member of the North Carolina Convention, "that a consolidated government will answer this country? *It is too large*."[10] In the Philadelphia Convention (1787) Mr. Dickinson, delegate from Delaware, laid stress on the importance of securing great powers to the States. "This," he said, "was the ground of his consolation for the future fate of his country. Without this, and in case of a consolidation of the States into one great Republic, we might read its fate in the history of the smaller ones."[11] This gentleman's colleague took a more searching glance into the future, and told the Convention, "Too much attachment is betrayed to the State governments. A national government must soon

---

[9] Speech of a member of the North Carolina Convention, Elliot's 'Debates,' iv. p. 51.

[10] Ibid. p. 24. Upon how narrow a basis the original Convention constructed the Union is shown by the remark of Mr. Sherman, that "there was no probability that the number of future States would exceed that of the existing States. If the event should ever happen, it was too remote to be taken into consideration at this time." (Madison's 'Reports,' p. 310.) Scarcely *eighty* years have passed, and the original number of States is already nearly *trebled*.

[11] Madison's 'Reports,' 148.

of necessity swallow them all up."[12] But, returned Mr. Hamilton again, and the men who thought with him re-echoed his words, "The State governments possess inherent advantages which will ever give them an influence and ascendency over the national government, and will for ever preclude the possibility of Federal encroachments."[13] And Madison frequently declared his belief that there was more to be feared from the encroachments of State governments upon the Federal government than from encroachments the other way.[14]

This great controversy, beginning with the birth of the government, became more hopeless of solution or compromise whenever a settlement was attempted. It was manifestly not of a nature to admit of being determined by peaceable means. The pretensions of the rival powers could only be laid at rest by one conquering the other. For it would inevitably happen that Congress would enact laws which some States would regard as depriving them of their just rights, they would resist, and a revolution might be delayed but could not ultimately be averted. Jefferson described the State and Federal governments as "co-ordinate powers," but he was constrained to admit that circumstances might arise in which one would trespass upon the functions of the other. Then where was the pacifying medium? Who was to be umpire between the contestants? "A Conven-

---

[12] Madison's 'Reports,' p. 163.

[13] Elliot's 'Debates,' ii. 239. See also ibid., pp. 304, 353, 365-68, and 459-64.

[14] Madison's 'Reports,' pp. 221-22.

tion of States," answers Jefferson, "must be called to ascribe the doubtful power to that department which they may think best." But the remedy was beyond the reach of the people at the very moment they needed it. In a period of excitement and agitation some quick and ready mode of arbitration is indispensable, if peace is to be preserved. Now it is a tardy and cumbrous process to call a Convention of the States; and if at any time the question in dispute is one which affects large classes variously, the Convention even when called would never be found to agree. This can be proved by an arithmetical statement. The concurrence of three-fourths of the States is necessary to carry out a change in the Constitution. In the differences between the North and the South it is evident that three-fourths of the States never could at any time have been brought to agree upon a single point. In 1861 there were thirty-three States in the Union, of which eleven demanded the right to live in a separate Confederation. At least five or six other States were divided in opinion with respect to this claim, some of their inhabitants approving and some opposing it. The remainder refused to listen to it for a moment. How, then, was it possible to bring three-fourths of the whole number into accordance? Compromise had been tried until the very mention of farther compromise was almost sufficient to stir up a revolution. The eleven States then said, "We will fight to obtain our liberty;" and the majority, seeing that they must fight or yield, and knowing well that they could not yield without losing all, and seeing moreover that the constitutional provision for settling disputes had completely broken down, accepted the challenge and went into the field. What else could be done? The nineteen States would not yield a point; the fourteen were equally inflexible. Thus the Constitution practically furnished no other instrument for the settlement of national differences but the sword.

The peace of the country will be jeopardised in precisely the same manner whenever a question arises which a proportion of the States exceeding one-fourth are anxious to carry. They will be strong enough to resist constitutional amendments. A convention of the States can settle nothing. War must then be the only arbitrator between the disputants. The amendments to the Constitution made since 1861 have been effected, with one exception—that abolishing slavery—by excluding the eleven insurgent States from voting. States which had never committed the folly of withdrawing their representatives from Congress could not be so treated, and it is doubtful whether the precedent of altering the Constitution by the device of forcibly suppressing the minority will receive the sanction of coming generations. A settlement of this kind can never be deemed permanent. As the disorganised minority become stronger they will be more strenuous in their demands for the restoration of their prerogatives The only means by which their ultimate success could be prevented would be by keeping them in perpetual subjection. Slavery was abolished by the vote of the Slave States, but negro suffrage and the disfranchisement of white citizens was forced upon them against their will, and in undoubted contravention of the express guarantee of the Constitution that each State shall be allowed to choose its own form of suffrage. The right of conquest was urged as the justification for this and many similar measures, but it is one of the arguments of the victors which are only cogent while cannon may be brought up to enforce them.

It is not without envy that Americans compare their own Constitution, as concerns the emendatory power, with that of Great Britain. They see that Parliament can and does readily carry out such reforms as may be called for by the progress and increase of the people. There is open and fair discussion, and the right of decision is not placed in an impossible majority. The American method of Reform, as it is described by an American writer, "is so difficult that it can rarely be resorted to at all, and so dangerous that to use it would be only something better than civil war, for it would be likely to provoke one. It implies more intelligence, and more dispassionate calmness of deliberation, than is or can be possessed by any people."[15] This, then, is one detail of government in which the Constitution has not answered to the necessities or expectations of the

[15] 'The Trial of the Constitution.' By Sidney George Fisher (Philadelphia, 1862.)

people. When it was framed the country was distracted by feuds which it was intended to remove. It helped to increase them. It was based upon the assumption that local differences would die out. They have been exasperated and embittered by violent discussions, by the conviction that they are irremediable, and by the memory of a thousand wrongs, real or fancied, on both sides. John Quincy Adams was one of the statesmen who dreaded this loosening of what has been called, with a touch of irony as it might almost seem, "the fraternal tie." "Far better will it be," said he in 1839, "for the people of the disunited States to part in friendship from each other than to be held together by constraint." His remark shows how little he understood his own country. It is too ambitious to permit itself to be cut into fragments. A partition of the Union is not possible without a war, unless there should ever be a majority for secession. Then the minority could no more hold the discontented fast than the minority could escape from the grasp of the majority in 1861. "One flag, one people" is the formula which expresses the modern theory of American Republicanism. The Union before everything—before States, before the Constitution, before even liberty itself. For that idea the American people have submitted to be taxed as few nations have ever been taxed before, and for it they would willingly endure afresh the burdens which the bloody contest of four years visited upon them.

CHAPTER III.

THE EXECUTIVE.

IT has been often represented that the Executive Department of the United States government is the most powerful and the least under control known to any country. Although there were bounds prescribed in the Constitution beyond which the President could not pass, yet those bounds seemed too elastic for the public safety, and the most accomplished American statesmen and constitutional writers have expressed misgivings lest one day the liberties of the people should be invaded. Patrick Henry, in the early days of the Republic, declared his dread that the President "might easily become a king." "If," he said, "your American chief be a man of ambition and abilities, how easy it will be for him to render himself absolute!" It was unquestionably the intention of those who originally framed the government that the Executive should exercise a considerable, and to some degree an independent control over public affairs. Judge Story, among other commentators on the Constitution, justifies this upon the ground that a feeble Executive implies a feeble execution of the government, and a feeble execution is but another phrase for a bad execution. The direct source of the influence possessed by the President was the patronage in his gift, but in the first years of the government the full importance of this was not realised, because the patronage was administered with an honest regard to the public service. But that the President was strong, stronger than a constitutional ruler in other parts of the world, was a theory which has generally been accredited as a fact. Few public men in America have hesitated to express the opinion that the Executive office was so carefully and surely guarded that it would be easier for a President to exceed his proper functions than for the Legislative to trespass upon his prerogatives. Mr. Seward, a man of unrivalled information upon the machinery of his own government, once said to me, "We elect a king for four years, and give him absolute power within certain limits, which after all he can interpret for himself." This is a proposition which would no longer be maintained by any American statesman. Among the unlooked-for consequences of the great struggle between the North and the South is the determination of the principle that the Executive is weak as soon as it is arrayed against the Legislative and the strong bias of public opinion. It is never more than relatively strong. Its arm is paralysed for independent action when it can no longer summon two-thirds of each Legislative Chamber to its side. Whatever strength it possesses is derived exclusively from the true fountain of political power, the people. The fear that the head of the administration might suffer at the hands of the other departments of the government was not absent from the minds of the founders of the Constitution. Washington always impressed upon his contemporaries the importance of preserving the independence of the office beyond the reach of attack. He told Jefferson in 1790, during the progress of a controversy with reference to the assumption of State debts, "that the President was the centre, in which all administrative questions ultimately rested, and that all of us (meaning the Cabinet) should rally round him, and support, with joint efforts, measures approved by him." In the Convention of 1787 it was urged by many members that in order to preserve the Executive from undue interference it should have the right to exercise an absolute negative, for, it was said, "without such a self-defence the Legislature can at any moment sink it into non-existence."[1] But there was a still more numerous party which shrank back alarmed from the thought that the President might indeed become a King. They conceived that the President was already made too powerful. It might be the fate of the country to be absolutely ruled for four years by one man. He might be a bad, unscrupulous, ambitious man; and if he could overmaster the Legislature the whole business of the country would be

[1] Madison's 'Reports,' p. 151, and speech of Mr. Gouverneur Morris, p. 334.

stopped, and a yoke immeasurably more intolerable than that from which they had escaped would be placed upon their necks. The short term of office and the qualified veto were regarded as indispensable securities, and the actual strength of the office was left, like many other details of the scheme, to be tested by subsequent experiment.

The memorable events which set this question at rest for ever, and made it past dispute that the Legislative can absorb the chief functions of the Executive whenever it is able to secure the co-operation of the majority in the country, have only occurred since the war. There was always a doubt respecting what the President could or could not do. A determined man, skilfully disguising his encroachments, might go far beyond the limits which his predecessors reached, and which the Constitution seemed to mark out. The history of the administration of President Jackson presents an illustration of the liberties which may be taken by a resolute man, not deficient in tact, and watching narrowly the shifting current of public opinion. He carried out his projects partly by his dogged determination and strength of character, but more by the unscrupulous use which he made of the self-interests of others. He let corruption loose upon the land. Every public office was a bribe—every post in his gift was put up for sale in the market-place. By this device he defied Congress, and yet was never an unpopular man. People rather admired and laughed at his "smartness." He succeeded in his aims, but his success was not the means of permanently enlarging the power and authority of his office. He merely showed how the Presidency might be made all-powerful by the exercise of craft, cunning, and a quick appreciation of the popular will. And even Jackson himself, after carrying out his own measures in opposition to the Legislature, thought it judicious to make professions of his subserviency to that body. In his message of 1836 he said, "No one can be more deeply impressed than I am with the soundness of the doctrine which restrains and limits excutive discretion."

It was the lack of the perception of the inherent weakness of the Executive, and its liability to be paralysed by the Legislative, which was the original source of President Johnson's troubles. That error cost him his reputation, and prevented him from being of that service to a disordered country which his general capacities warranted his friends in expecting. He could not understand that he might be practically deposed. When he succeeded Mr. Lincoln he was wedded to a scheme which he had devised for the restoration of the Southern States, and he never once doubted his ability to carry it through. The language of his vetoes in 1866, though more guarded than his speeches, betrayed this belief in his supremacy, and it was one of the first circumstances which provoked the suspicions and hostility of the Republican party. They were incensed at his pretensions, and disappointed with the total change which he avowed in his opinions. On the 21st of April, 1865, he told a delegation from Indiana that "treason against the government of the United States is the highest crime that can be committed, and those engaged in it should suffer all its penalties." And again he said, "traitors must be made odious, treason must be made odious, and traitors must be punished and impoverished." Their "social power must be destroyed," and "every Union man and the government should be remunerated out of the pockets of those who have inflicted this great suffering upon the country."

It was no wonder that the Republican party should at first have placed almost unlimited faith and confidence in the man who took every occasion to utter sentiments such as these. They thought they saw the "hand of God" in the "removal" of Mr. Lincoln and the substitution of a man of sterner mould. But Mr. Johnson had not been long in office before the facts which were brought to his knowledge, as chief of the nation, convinced him that the South needed no additional stripes to reduce it to submission. Its load was already greater than it could bear. The President's compassion was moved by the great and ceaseless cry of misery and despair which every breeze carried to him from across the Potomac. As he looked from his windows in the White House towards the South, he saw a country which was entirely given over to its enemies, and which could look only to him for aid. He thought it was his duty as the Executive to stand by the States which had sinned and repented, and which now demanded his protection. But Mr. Johnson was not free from the Southern inflammability of temperament, and the gibes of his political antagonists unfortunately excited him to make open war upon the Legislative. Misled by his belief that almost unlimited power was intrusted to him, he sought opportunities to attack Congress when ordinary discretion might have admonished him to act on the defensive. He spoke of that body as "hanging on the verge of the government," "traitors at the other end of the line," "the tail of the government," and used other terms which denoted that in his opinion he possessed the chief, and Congress only a secondary right, to direct public affairs. The people were alarmed at this language, and deeply offended by the want of dignity and self-command which the President occasionally displayed. In this respect Americans are not less sensitive than the older and more aristocratic nations of the world. They expect their chief magistrate to comport himself in a manner becoming the head of a great people. They may choose him from a humble rank, but they look to him to rise to the level of the post in which they place him. Mr. Johnson's constant allusions to his original calling were excessively distasteful to the people. They considered that he dishonoured himself and his office by haranguing every crowd which chose to bring a barbarous band of music under his windows, and yell forth vulgar songs, and scream for "Andy Johnson." They were ashamed to find their chief magistrate bandying slang and interchanging coarse personalities with the scourings of the streets and the ruffians of the bar-room. They smarted under the sense that they were degraded in the eyes of the world, and that a great crisis in their affairs was made to look puerile and mean. It was useless for Mr. Johnson to boast of his humble origin and his early struggles. The nation took no pride in them. An American writer well expressed the common feeling of his countrymen when he remarked—"The people do not take it as a compliment to be told that they have chosen a plebeian to the highest office, for they are not fond of a plebeian tone of mind or manners. What they do like, we believe, is to be represented by their foremost man, their highest type of courage, sense, and patriotism, no matter what his origin."[2] But it was with strange forgetfulness of the very root of all their political and social theories that the President's origin was cast in his teeth as an insult. The coarseness of these attacks sometimes shocked men of all parties. "His head," said a member of the House, at a public meeting in Washington,[3] "will rest more quietly on the lapboard and the goose than while oppressed with a crown." It was a mistake on the part of the President to dwell so much upon the

[2] 'North American Review,' April 1866.

[3] Held 3rd December, 1866. The speaker was Mr. Covode, of Pennsylvania.

past, but it was cowardice in his opponents to make it matter of reproach against him. They had not been deceived. They chose with their eyes open. They knew who and what Mr. Johnson was before they elected him Vice-President. If the people do not like mechanics to be their great public officers, they need not go to that class for them. But the truth is, that many of the results of popular government are unsatisfactory to the Americans when they are brought into close contact with them. They would not for the world renounce the principle that all men are equal; but they would give a great deal to make their principle harmonise with facts.

The differences between the President and the Legislature soon became irreconcilable. Mr. Johnson thoroughly believed that Congress was exceeding its proper functions in refusing to adopt his or some similar plan for the speedy admission of the eleven insurgent States; and yet nothing can be more firmly established than the right of each House to decide for itself upon the qualifications of its members. This was a province in which the Executive had no right to interfere. But Mr. Johnson was eager to restore the Southern States to their former position, honestly believing that representation in the national legislature belonged to them of right, and that it was to the interest of the country that they should possess it soon and unabridged. The majority in Congress contended that the Secessionists had forfeited their former claim to representation, and could only be received afresh into the Legislature upon new terms, such terms as their conquerors chose to insist on. Then arose the charge and countercharge of "centralization" and "oppression." Members of Congress standing up in their places stigmatised the President as a tyrant, a despot, and an usurper. He was even accused of conspiring with the assassin Booth, a low theatrical madman, to murder Mr. Lincoln. The most intolerable accusations were levelled at his private character. Mr. Johnson retorted upon his assailants in a similar temper, and in language not less violent than that which proceeded from their lips. He made his appeal to the country through his veto messages, and the answer was returned by the re-election of the Congress which had passed its Bills over his vetoes, and thus reduced him to the position of a mere agent who feebly protests against measures which he is bound to put into execution with his own hand.

All these events proved that the power of the Executive is very limited, and that what little of it there is depends upon the will of the people. Popular or unpopular, the President stands practically unsupported. He is the Minister of Congress, a chief magistrate, not an independent ruler. No man occupying the Presidential chair can hope to carry out his own views or measures when Congress is confirmed in its opposition to him by the majority of the people. His blindness to this unwritten law was another of the errors into which Mr. Johnson fell, and it was one which added to the misfortunes of the Southern States. The Northern people, angered at the zeal and ardour of their partizan, became more and more embittered against those who had endeavoured to destroy the Union. The generous impulse of forgiveness which immediately succeeded the war soon passed away. The President was determined to bring the South back into the Union upon what he deemed just, and what undoubtedly were strictly constitutional, conditions. He did not take into consideration several circumstances which might have been sufficient to warn him that failure beset his steps. During the war unusual, and even unconstitutional, powers had been wielded by the Executive. The liberty of the press was sometimes interrupted, and private citizens were arrested, as Mr. Seward said, upon the tinkling of a little bell. These and a hundred other arbitrary acts were condoned by the people in consideration of the perils to the government which they were designed to ward off or avenge. The war came to an end; Mr. Lincoln died; and his successor thought to exercise the same authoritative sway which had been sanctioned in the hour of the nation's trial and extremity. He did not perceive that an absolutism which was justifiable in time of war would not be submitted to in time of peace. Congressional rule, which had sunk into comparative abeyance, was sure to be revived. The Legislative, which had to a certain extent been subverted, began to recover its former place. The issue was invited by the President himself whether Congress or the Executive should govern the country, and the people decided in favour of Congress. The President had apparently grasped at a dictatorship to which he was not deemed to be entitled, either by precedent, the Constitution, or by extraordinary qualities of personal fitness. Mr. Lincoln, covered with the glory of the war, could not have carried out what Mr. Johnson attempted. Instead of keeping the Southern States in the position in which they had placed themselves by the war until Congress met in December, 1865, or instead of calling an earlier and extra session, he proceeded to "reconstruct" them according to his own method. In somewhat peremptory terms he urged Congress to follow the course upon which he had entered, and to receive the Southern delegates into their midst. But the members of both Houses met him in an incensed mood. Their first act was to assemble in private and form committees to which all questions affecting the return of the seceded States to Congress should be referred. In vain the President interposed his vetoes, and declaimed from the steps of the White House, or appealed to the multitude in a journey through the West. The people heard him coldly, even contemptuously. The constant cry which met his ears was, "We will not be robbed of our victory—the South shall never make another attempt to divide the Union." The President would not be convinced that it was the true voice of the people which he heard. The elections of 1866 might have removed his doubts, but they seemed only to confirm him in his inflexibility, and his message to the second session of the thirty-ninth Congress contained the avowal that he had not changed his convictions, but that on the contrary time had confirmed his belief in their correctness.

The disagreement between the Executive and the Legislative was too fundamental to admit of a compromise. Both Houses met on the 3rd of December, 1866, fully determined to reduce the Presidential authority to a shadow, and afterwards to force Mr. Johnson to carry into effect their own policy. The threat of impeachment was constantly held over his head without making the least impression upon a nature so unbending and determined. The first attack made was upon the Executive right of patronage. This had always been a subject of controversy. In the early stages of the government, the patronage in the gift of the President was very considerable. The growth of the country, and the multiplication of offices, has rendered it enormous. When Judge Story wrote his Commentaries upon the Constitution, in 1840, he was already impressed with the belief that the exercise of this patronage might become "one of the most dangerous and corrupt engines to destroy private independence and public liberty which can assail the Republic." In whom the power to remove public officers was vested by the Constitution has never been properly decided. If the Senate, 't was argued by some, could alone confirm and perfect appointments, so that body alone could put a termination to them. The Congress of 1798 seemed to decide that the power of removal rested with the President, but the decision has ever been deemed questionable and unsatisfactory. Nevertheless, successive Presidents continued to claim this privilege.[4] Some of them used it as an engine of corruption, and one or two pushed it to the verge of recklessness. The mischief to be caused now by the same conduct is much greater than it was in former times. An able American writer, Professor Bowen, has justly described the magnitude of the evil:—"The patronage of the President of the United States," he remarks, "is now enormous, and has become a dominant feature in the operation of our national government. Reckoning the subordinate officers in the Post-office and Customs departments, all of whom derive their appointments directly or indirectly from the President, and continue in office only during his pleasure, and most of whom, in fact, give place to new incumbents at every change of administration, it is easy to see that the influence of the Executive government, through the number of places at its disposal, has become excessive, and imperils both the moral character and the stability of our republican institutions."

---

[4] Story explained how all checks upon the exercise of this privilege might be evaded. (See Story, p. 175, small ed.)

[5] Professor Bowen's note to 'De Tocqueville,' pp. 157-58. In quoting the English translation of M. de Tocqueville's work th

During the recess of 1866 this tremendous weapon was used freely by President Johnson in the hope of controlling the autumn elections. Public officers of republican principles were removed in order to make room for men pledged to support the administration. This stroke produced an effect the reverse of that which was anticipated. The President's party secured indeed the votes of the new functionaries, but the indignation of the bulk of the people was aroused at the abuse of patronage, exaggerated as it was by the reports of the hostile party, and they came forward in a solid phalanx against the author of it. Thus encouraged, Congress on the very first day of meeting received several proposals from its members to restrict the appointing power in the hands of the President. The most important of them was introduced by Mr. Stevens in the form of a Bill to "regulate removals from office." It provided that removals from office should be made only with the consent of the Senate; that the President should have power to suspend from their duties incompetent or defaulting officers during the recess of the Senate, but only upon condition that within ten days after the next meeting of the Senate the Pre-

---

author has used the excellent edition published by Professor Bowen, founded on Mr. Henry Reeves's, and published at Cambridge (U.S.) 1864. For the convenience of the reader the reference is also given to the corresponding passage in the original text, the edition quoted throughout being the fourteenth, published by Michel Lévy Frères, 1865.

sident "shall submit his reasons for the removal of any officer to that body, and in case they are not concurred in the inculpated person shall be restored to his position;" that every person recommended to the Senate for office, and rejected, "shall be incapable of holding any office under the United States for the term of three years after such rejection, unless two-thirds of the Senate shall relieve him of such disability." And the Bill further made it imperative upon the President to submit all his nominations to the Senate within twenty days after they were made, or after the commencement of the next succeeding session of the Senate.

Such was the first of the measures which were destined to strike at the very root of the illicit influence which the Executive possessed. It was soon surpassed by more sweeping propositions. There was much to be said in favour of these proceedings. The system of corruption which has been developed in the United States by the disposal of patronage is universal. Office-seekers throng the ante-rooms of the White House every day, and once in every four years, when a change of President occurs, the majority of men in public offices have always been liable to dismissal. The disadvantages occasioned to the public service are incalculable. Men are chosen to fill posts, not on account of their fitness, but because of the service they have been or may be in elections. It is no honour to be a member of the Civil Service in America. It is best to allow an American writer to explain the opinions of his countrymen upon this subject.[6] "The Government rarely finds itself able to secure the best men for its civil service. . . . So that we witness at this moment the extraordinary fact, that to be the servant of what is fondly called 'the best government the world ever saw,' not only does not, as in other countries, raise a man in the social scale, but actually reflects something very like discredit on him." And the writer goes on to say that "waste, corruption, inefficiency, and want of discipline," are the consequences of this system.

It cannot be doubted, then, that there was great need for the reform pressed by the Republican party in 1866. They proposed it for purposes of party; they were naturally unwilling to see the whole patronage of the government taken away from them and conferred upon the opposition, while they were all-powerful and the opposition was but an insignificant minority; but still their recommendation had so much intrinsic justice in it that it was willingly accepted by the people. It could not be alleged that it was a novel attack upon the prerogatives assumed by the Executive. In the Congress of 1789 there had been a long discussion upon the appointing power of the President, and it was contended that it might "render the Chief Magistrate arbitrary, and, in some measure, absolute." That Congress, as I

[6] 'North American Review,' July, 1865.

have stated, left the question undecided, and it does not appear to have been revived in the Legislature until 1826, when on the 4th of May Colonel Benton presented a report from a Committee of the House of Representatives, to the effect that the amount of patronage exercised by the President ought to be reduced by law, and presenting six Bills for that purpose. No action was taken upon them, and the subject was again neglected until the session of 1834-35, when a Committee of the Senate was appointed to inquire into the expediency of reducing the Executive patronage. A long report was subsequently presented by this committee, of which Mr. Calhoun was chairman, and a Bill was brought in which required the President to assign his reasons to Congress for the removal of any officer. In the debate upon this measure Mr. Webster delivered one of his great speeches, in which he contended that the framers of the Constitution never intended to give the President the power of removing public servants from office.[7] The Bill was passed, but the system of corruption it was intended to destroy continued to grow, and to inflict year after year greater evils upon the country. At last, in the early part of 1867, a Bill passed both Houses[8] which ren-

[7] 'Works of Daniel Webster' (Boston, 1866), vol. iv. p. 179.

[8] Known as the 'Tenure of Office Bill.' It seems impossible that this law can stand. During the recess of Congress a man proved to be guilty of theft or forgery may be in a public office, and the President be powerless to remove him until the Senate meet. Moreover, it is manifestly contrary to the interests of the public service that the President should not be free to choose his own Cabinet.

dered the President incompetent either to remove or appoint public officers of the higher grades, or even his Cabinet Ministers, without the consent and approval of the Senate. It was vetoed by Mr. Johnson, but re-passed instantly and became the law of the land.

Every event in the course of this long struggle proved that a President of the United States cannot be strong unless he consents to obey the behests of a powerful party. Mr. Johnson had separated himself from the party which caused his election, and the other side were too doubtful about his principles to adopt him as their representative. Besides, he came to them with an injured reputation, and they had already more than enough odium to bear in consequence of their opposition to the war. It is doubtful whether when all the States are fully represented any future President can be as weak as Mr. Johnson found himself. But the Executive must necessarily always be dependent upon party, and much at the mercy of the Legislature. The single circumstance that the occupant of the office is liable to impeachment and trial by the body upon which it is a part of his duty to exercise a check must suffice to keep him in subjection. He must be the creature of those who nominated him. He will be judged by the fidelity with which he has adhered to his friends and supporters. Just before Mr. Lincoln's death he gave indications of being animated by more merciful feelings towards the insurrectionary States than his political friends approved. Instantly they turned round angrily upon him, and denounced his conduct with a readiness and violence which showed how little past services avail when a public officer ceases to do the bidding of his party. Any man who entered upon the Presidency with his mind imbued with the precepts of the Constitution, and the teaching of the "Fathers," would ruin his cause and himself in a twelvemonth.

The condition to which the Presidential office has fallen is a memorable instance of the fallacy of theories of government. Upon this part of their system the founders of the Constitution lavished endless study and care. They had the experience of the world to guide them, and they believed that they were about to advance the science of government a thousand years. But their favourite piece of work has disappointed the people. The Executive is a prize contended for chiefly by hungry place-hunters, or by the obscure and illiterate puppets of a faction. The educated class has been driven from the ranks of competitors. The office has almost ceased to be an object of ambition, and the holder of it must, by the inevitable circumstances of his position, be the slave of those who set him in the place of authority, only to use him for their own purposes. He is kept upon a stinted allowance, and for four years is the butt and jeer of the party opposed to his own. After his term of office is fulfilled he sinks into sudden obscurity and contempt. An ex-President is a ruined man.

He is less thought of, less regarded, than the most commonplace of politicians. He is seldom seen in society; scarcely is he ever spoken of by the public press without a sneering adjective prefixed to his name. All sections of all parties carefully avoid him, because he is sure to have done something to offend some class in the country whose influence is needed at elections. All this is a strange contrast to that imaginary Executive which Madison and his contemporaries had before their eyes. They meant the post to be one full of dignity and honour, but, among many other miscalculations, they failed to make allowance for the deteriorating effect of an almost unrestricted suffrage. They trusted too much to the continual existence of a Conservative tendency in a community which was told that it might recast the fabric of its government whenever it was in the humour.

The re-eligibility of the President may be one cause of the gradual decadence of the office. It is now to the interest of the minority to blacken and defame him so that he at least may be removed from their path. It is also to the interest of the President to scheme and manœuvre for a second term. President Jackson, in his first annual message, suggested that the period of service of the chief magistrate should be limited to a single term of either four or six years, and from the time of the Federal Convention until now the same idea has constantly been a subject of discussion. The chief objections to it are those mentioned by Mr. Justice Story—namely, that it would deprive the country of the experience gained by the chief magistrate in the exercise of office, and that "it might banish men from the station in certain emergencies, in which their services might be eminently useful, and indeed almost indispensable for the safety of their country."[9] But if the period of office were extended from four to seven years these possible inconveniences would be guarded against, and the great evils of constantly recurring Presidential elections, with all the demoralization and excitement which they bring, would be modified. The time is probably approaching when some change of this kind will be made. Some steps towards it have already been taken. On the 11th of February, 1867, a debate arose in the Senate upon a proposition to amend the Constitution in order that the President might be made ineligible for re-election. To this an amendment was moved making his term of office six instead of four years, and two of the leading senators, representing the Republican and Democratic parties,[10] spoke upon the question. The Democratic member thought that there would be no danger in enlarging the term of office, and the Republican recommended a still greater change in the Constitution — namely, that the President be chosen directly by the people without the intervention of

[9] 'Commentaries,' 1442-1449.

[10] Senators Sumner (Massachusetts), and Reverdy Johnson (Maryland).

Electoral Colleges. "Such an amendment," he said, "would give to every individual voter, wherever he might be, a certain weight in the election." He might have added that it would abolish a clumsy wheel in the great machinery of corruption which is set going at the time of a Presidential election.[11]

---

[11] MODE OF ELECTING THE PRESIDENT.—The persons whose votes elect the President are chosen by the people at large. Each State has as many electors as it returns Senators and Representatives to Congress, but no member of Congress, or officer of the United States drawing any emolument, is eligible to vote for the President. The electors meet in their own States, on the first Wednesday in December in every fourth year succeeding the last election, and vote by ballot for President and Vice-President. A list is then made of the candidates and the number of votes recorded for each, and sealed up and transmitted to the President of the Senate, before the first Wednesday of January following the election. On the second Wednesday of February the President of the Senate, in the presence of both Houses of Congress, opens the list, counts the votes, and declares the result. If no one candidate has gained a majority of the total number of electors, the five highest on the list are selected, and from one of this number the House of Representatives immediately elects a President by ballot. In such an extraordinary election one representative from each State votes. In case of the death of the President, or his unfitness for office, the Vice-President succeeds him, and serves out the remainder of the term for which the President was elected. Should the Vice-President also die or be incapacitated, the Speaker of the House would perform the duties of the Executive until the next election. The only qualifications for President are that he must be a natural-born citizen, or a citizen of the United States at the time of the adoption of the Constitution, that he shall be not less than thirty-five years of age, and have been fourteen years a resident of the United States. He is elected for four years, is allowed 25,000 dollars a year and a residence at Washington, and he is eligible for re-election.

Mr. Justice Story points out a curious omission in the Constitution. "No provision," he says, "seems to be made, or at least directly made, for the case of the non-election of any President or Vice-President at the period prescribed by the Constitution. The case of a vacancy by removal, death, or resignation, is expressly provided for; but not of a vacancy by the expiration of the official term of office." He quotes another learned commentator who remarks that the oversight may be of use when the people are weary of the Constitution and government, and desire to put an end to both—"a mode of dissolution which seems, from its peaceable character, to recommend itself to his mind as fit for such a crisis." But Mr. Justice Story points out that the failure of an election would amount to nothing more than a temporary suspension of the functions of the Executive, and there cannot be a doubt that the Legislative would quickly provide for this or any other emergency that might arise.

CHAPTER IV.

THE CABINET.

IN the government at Washington the Secretaries and Ministers hold a position altogether different from that which is occupied by the advisers of the Crown in constitutional Europe. There Parliamentary business is conducted by the Cabinet, while in America the Cabinet is in reality merely a Board of heads of departments. It works in the dark, and is not allowed the opportunity of taking any part in the discussion of public affairs. Its members cannot sit in either branch of the Legislature; and when the administration finds it necessary to secure the passage of a particular measure, not having a duly authorised representative in Congress, it employs any mouthpiece which offers itself, or which is disposed to take a reward for serving it. This is an engine of corruption which is forced upon the use of the government, for there are times when circumstances compel it to offer bribes for support, even in the advocacy of measures which are essential to the public service, but which Congress may be disposed to evade or postpone. Then some member of influence in the House is needed to press the subject upon the attention of his colleagues, to "call up" the Bill, whatever it may be, to bring forward the arguments in its favour, to answer objections, and to see that it is not killed by the introduction of dilatory resolutions — that system of tactics which is called in Congressional language "filibustering." The advocate must necessarily receive his instructions from the department of government which is immediately interested in the measure, and it is seldom that he expects or is expected to take his trouble for nothing. If a member of Congress desires information with regard to any events which may be transpiring, he cannot put a question to any Minister in the House, but he goes instead to the proper office of State, and his vote is usually of sufficient consequence to gain for him a ready audience with the Secretary. Indeed, office doors stand perpetually open in Washington. The government establishments are accessible to all persons, no matter on what errand they may be bound; and a Minister is seldom so firmly grounded in the confidence of the nation as to be able to afford himself the luxury of doing his work in private, undisturbed by the crowd of idlers whose only claim upon him rests in the fact that they belong to his party.

The Cabinet in America has been solely the creation of party. The Constitution makes no mention of it as a *Cabinet*, and refers but slightly to the heads of departments; while the commentators do not appear to have given any attention to the subject. It consists of seven members, each of whom is wholly destitute of influence except in the department placed under his charge. Each receives a salary of $8000 a year. It has always been the custom for the President to choose his advisers, and to change them whenever he thought proper, without any virtual restraint or hindrance, and this privilege has been used without question by every President, from Washington to Lincoln. But in 1867, as it has been said in a previous chapter, Congress took advantage of the personal unpopularity of President Johnson to strike away this function of the Executive in order that its power in the administration might not be weakened. There have been Presidents who changed their Cabinets entirely more than once, because of differences of opinion, and no one dreamt of denying the propriety or expediency of the step. But for the future, unless the law of 1867 be rescinded, the President will have merely a secondary voice in the selection of his Ministers. Unless the Senate approve the men whom he may wish to appoint, or agree to the removal of those whom he may desire to displace, the chief posts in the public departments may be kept vacant. The President may still suspend his Ministers and nominate their successors; the Senate may refuse to confirm the latter, and thus the whole powers of the Executive may be represented exclusively by the chief.

This is one of those changes in the construction of the government which no law forbade, but which were in the last degree ill-considered and unadvisable. It was adopted from party motives, to serve certain purposes of the hour, and the authors of it may hereafter have reason to repent sincerely of their work. It is only reasonable that the President for the time being should have the benefit of the advice of men in whose judgment he has confidence. It is not for the public benefit to surround him with counsellors whose advice he will constantly reject, and who will turn the Council-room into a scene of incessant disputes and contention. The Cabinet was never designed to be a check upon the President, and it has no power within it to enable it to struggle successfully against him. The Ministers cannot act without his sanction, except in so far as they are supported by express laws, but he can act without them. An experienced and really valuable public servant will rarely be removed by the incoming President, who naturally desires to gain all the useful aid he can in the execution of his duties. President Lincoln's Cabinet was for a long time retained almost intact by his successor, although some of the members of it were extremely obnoxious to President Johnson. A few of them found that they could bring their minds into harmony with his views, several retired, and one was expelled from his office after an undignified attempt to keep possession in defiance of the head of the government. The Secretary of War had rendered himself peculiarly distasteful to the President by a course of opposition which was never modified for a moment, and which was not always respectful in its nature. He sat at the Council Board only to condemn every suggestion made by the President, often in language which is said to have been calculated to arouse the ire of a less impulsive man than Mr. Johnson. At last the President wrote a note to him in which he was requested to resign. The Secretary curtly declined.[1] In this position what was to be done? Was the President still to receive in his rooms the Minister who had treated him and his authority with contempt? Was he still to be advised by the public servant whom he had discharged? The business of the

---

[1] The following is a copy of the correspondence:—

Executive Mansion, Washington, August 5, 1867.

To EDWIN M. STANTON, Secretary of War:—

SIR,—Grave public considerations constrain me to request your resignation as Secretary of War.

ANDREW JOHNSON,
President of the United States.

War Department, Washington, August 6, 1867.

To his Excellency ANDREW JOHNSON, President of the United States:—

SIR,—Your note informing me that grave public considerations constrain you to request my resignation as Secretary of War has been received. In answer I have to state that grave public considerations constrain me to continue in the office of Secretary of War until the next meeting of Congress.

EDWIN M. STANTON,
Secretary of War.

country could not be carried on in this spirit; and as the President had decided upon the removal of his refractory counsellor, it was imperative upon him to insist on being obeyed. The Secretary went out under protest, and the Senate was left to take up the struggle in his behalf at its next meeting.

No one had ever anticipated such events as these. When the position of Ministers of State was discussed in the first Congress, Mr. Madison contended that a President would never dare to remove a faithful public servant; but that this was nothing more than a personal impression is proved by the fact just stated that Washington himself did remove Ministers who were not even charged with any want of capacity or neglect of duty, and that all his successors imitated his example. As a general rule this plan cannot be unpopular. The President will represent the governing party, and of course he will nominate as his subordinates in the executive government men holding similar opinions to his own. But if the governing party should turn out to be forsaken by their candidate, or deceived in him, they will be injured by the operation of a system which was devised for party purposes, and will only act well at a time when there is a natural balance of parties. A President who turns the weapons of office against those who elected him will necessarily be a thorn in their sides in every exercise of his authority. It is one of the penalties of making an indiscreet or an unfortunate choice. But it is a mistake to set aside every precedent and violate every rule in order to provide a cure for an evil which is only of a temporary character.

There is no such thing, then, as Cabinet government in the United States, although of late there has been a tendency to make each individual Minister responsible for the actions of the Executive. If this were carried to its complete result it would prevent the necessity of a President expelling froward members from his Cabinet, by leading them to withdraw when they discovered the impossibility of agreeing with him. If they were to be held responsible for his acts, they would hasten to set themselves right with the people by resigning their offices. This would be in accordance with the theories of Federal government, which support the claim of the rulers to all the prizes of office—the contest for the Presidency determining all minor struggles for four years. The party which is in possession of the majority is never likely to reconcile itself to the loss of all the chief positions in the country. Through the heads of departments the patronage is distributed, and the minority will therefore very seldom be allowed to retain a hold upon them.

But still it is possible for the Ministers of State to hold office for many years together, and in this there is often a great advantage to the public. The head of a department has time and opportunity to acquaint himself thoroughly with his duties, to become familiar with all the ramifications to which his office extends, to introduce and persevere in a definite policy, without the fear hanging over his head of a sudden removal on account of an adverse vote in the Legislature. Congress as a body has no jurisdiction over him, and by the Tenure of Office Bill the President and the Senate combined could not displace him. He must remain in office during the term of the Executive who appointed him. No doubt a total change of party majority would be almost certain to lead to a change in the Cabinet, but Ministers do not necessarily go out upon the election of a new President. The American navy, for instance, was controlled throughout the war by the same man, and it was under his direction that the fleet was entirely remodelled. His plans were not upset by the return of an adverse party to power, and the successor of Mr. Lincoln did not think it necessary to interfere with him. Mr. Lincoln's Foreign Secretary still remains in office, and his Financial Secretary might have done so likewise if he had not resigned on a question of patronage.[2] Under any circumstances which may arise the Ministers are free from the direct criticism of the Legislature. They are not under the terror of being cross-questioned upon delicate subjects in troubled times by impatient members. They are not called upon

---

[2] Mr. Lincoln wished to place his own supporters in the Treasury Department; Mr. Chase considered that he should be left free to choose his subordinates on grounds independent of their political convictions· and as they could not agree, the Secretary resigned.

to undergo the fatigue and exertion of attendance in Congress. They have their whole time to devote to the every-day duties of their respective offices, and there is not one of them who does not work as hard as any of his clerks.

It is usual for the President to consult with the Cabinet upon all questions of public interest, but he uses his own discretion with regard to following their advice. *He* is responsible for all his acts—not they. An eminent Minister once told me that these Cabinet meetings are ordinarily very simple and formal in their character. They are held once a week, at the White House, the residence of the President. The President sits at the head of the table, and asks the secretary of each department whether he has any business to bring forward. If he has any he says so, and produces his papers or notes, and the matter is discussed. Should there be a difference of opinion, the question is put to the vote, and the action which the majority desire is usually taken. But the Minister to whom I refer informed me[3] that there is seldom any disagreement upon departmental affairs, and in all other matters the President can, if he please, come to a decision without going through the form of consulting the Cabinet. On occasions when some question of grave importance has required a settlement the President, since the

[3] This was in 1865. After the differences between Mr. Johnson and his Cabinet, he would probably give a different account.

war, has been in the habit of calling in to the council-board, by special invitation, the General in command of the army, who gives his opinion with the rest. But this was a proceeding dictated by the personal popularity of the officer in question, and cannot be drawn into a precedent for future usage.

CHAPTER V.

THE LEGISLATIVE.

WE have seen that the Executive is destitute of all influence or power in framing the laws of the United States. As Chancellor Kent explains his functions, he has no discretion left to him in the execution of the laws made by a body which is entirely independent of him. "It is not for him to deliberate and decide upon the wisdom or expediency of the law. What has been once declared to be law, under all the cautious forms of deliberation prescribed by the Constitution, ought to receive prompt obedience."[1] The law-making power is vested exclusively in Congress, consisting of the Senate and the House of Representatives.

The constitution of the Senate is simple. Each State in the Union, regardless of its population or area, is entitled to send two members to this body. The House of Representatives is constructed upon a different plan. The Constitution originally directed that to the whole number of free persons in each

[1] 'Commentaries on American Law,' Part II. Lect. xiii. (The edition quoted in this book is the eleventh, published at Boston, 1866.)

State three-fifths of all other persons, excluding Indians not taxed, should be added, and representatives divided according to the population, not more than one representative being allowed for every 30,000 persons. On May 29, 1850, this plan was abolished, and it was provided that after March, 1853, the House of Representatives should be composed of 233 members, who are apportioned in the following manner:—The aggregate population of the United States, according to the last official census, is divided by 233, and the product is taken as the ratio or rule of apportionment. The population of each State is then taken, and divided by the ratio just determined, and the representatives allotted in accordance with the result.[2] The senators are chosen by the votes of the State Legislatures; the representatives by the direct suffrages of the people. The entire House of Representatives is elected at various times, for two years; the six years' term of office of senators is so arranged as that one-third only shall fall vacant every second year, so that, while it is possible for the people to change the entire House of Representatives once in two years, they cannot touch more than one-third of the Senate in the same time. "This provision," remarks Chancellor Kent, "is admirably calculated, on the one hand, to infuse into the Senate, biennially, renewed

[2] Territories are allowed to send two delegates to the House of Representatives. They may speak in the assembly, but are not permitted to vote.

public confidence and vigour; and, on the other, to retain a large portion of experienced members, duly initiated into the general principles of national policy, and the forms and course of business in the House."[3]

Thus, then, the Legislative is divided into two bodies, each having a control over the other, and the concurrence of both being requisite to make laws. The popular branch was intended to be the direct representative of the people, the Senate of the people incorporated as States, all the States returning through their Legislatures the same number of senators irrespective of their area, wealth, or population.[4] By this double contrivance it was thought that no class or interest in the country would be left without its due share of representation in the councils of the nation. The precise ends which the founders of the Constitution aimed to accomplish will be most satisfactorily explained by a brief reference to the expounders of it "It is the people only," said President Adams in his inaugural address, "that are represented: it is their power and majesty that is

---

[3] 'Commentaries,' Part II. Lect. xi.

[4] It was the original design that the Senate should be a check upon the popular power. Thus, in the Convention of 1787, Mr. Randolph said,—"He observed that the general object was to provide for the evils under which the United States laboured; that in tracing these evils to their origin, every man had found it in the turbulence and follies of democracy; that some check therefore was to be sought for against this tendency of our government; and that a good Senate seemed most likely to answer the purpose." (Madison's Reports,' p. 138.)

reflected, and only for their good in every legitimate government under whatever form it may appear." According to Jefferson the guiding principle of representation should be to secure the absolute supremacy of the will of the majority. In his inaugural address he insists upon the importance of "absolute acquiescence in the decisions of the majority, the vital principle of republics, from which there is no appeal but to force." In a letter to a friend he remarks,— "My most earnest wish is to see the republican element of popular control pushed to the maximum of its practical exercise. I shall then believe that our government may be pure and perpetual."[5] And again he writes,—"The first principle of republicanism is that the *lèx majoris partis* is the fundamental law of every society of individuals of equal rights; to consider the will of the society enounced by the majority of a single vote as sacred as if unanimous, is the first of all lessons in importance, yet the last which is thoroughly learnt."[6] There have been writers who openly contended that there would be no danger in giving the whole control of the government to the Legislative. "The old Congress," says one,[7] "held the Executive power of the Union. It was a plural Executive, annually appointed, liable to recall, ineligible after three years. . . . A sovereignty

[5] Jefferson's Works, vol. vii. p. 32. [6] Ibid. vol. vii. p. 75.

[7] John Taylor, a Virginian: 'Inquiry into the principles and policy of the Government of the United States' (1848), pp. 175 and 211.

over the Constitution, objectionable as it would still be, would be safer in the Legislature than in the Judiciary, because of its duennial responsibility." But there can be no question that those who drew up the Constitution attached great importance to the principle that each department of the government should be kept distinct from the others, and independent of them. "To what purpose," says Hamilton, "separate the Executive or the Judiciary from the Legislative, if both the Executive and the Judiciary are so constituted as to be at the absolute devotion of the Legislative? Such a separation must be merely nominal, and incapable of producing the ends for which it was established."[8] The only men who seem to have been desirous of placing the preponderance of power in the hands of the Legislative were those who represented the section of the country which suffered most by that change in after years.

The powers possessed by Congress are specifically defined by the Constitution.[9] It is authorised to levy and collect taxes, to borrow money, to regulate commerce with foreign nations, to coin money and regulate the value thereof, to constitute tribunals inferior to the Supreme Court, to declare war and to raise and support armies, to maintain a navy, and make rules for the regulation of the land and naval forces, to admit new States to Congress, and make laws for the regulation of territories,[10] and to exercise

[8] 'Federalist,' No. 71. [9] Art. I. sect. 8. [10] Art. IV. sect. 3.

exclusive legislation over the district which is the seat of the Government of the United States.[11] By an amendment to the original Constitution it is provided that "Congress shall make no law respecting an establishment of religion, or prohibiting the free exercise thereof; or abridging the freedom of speech, or of the press; or the right of the people peaceably to assemble, and to petition the government for a redress of grievances." Chancellor Kent remarks of the powers thus committed to Congress, that some of them, "as the levying of taxes, duties, and excises, are concurrent with similar powers in the several States; but in most cases these powers are exclusive, because the concurrent exercise of them by the States separately would disturb the general harmony and peace, and because they would be apt to be repugnant to each other in practice and lead to dangerous collisions." We shall see hereafter that Congress has always shown a disposition to enlarge the sphere of its authority, and to transcend the plain and express provisions of the Constitution. It was inevitable that this should happen. Congress, with the support of the majority to maintain it, was sure to gain the ascendency in the State. That it should always retain in the framework of government precisely the position assigned to it in the Constitu-

---

[11] It was in the exercise of this last power that Congress finally passed an Act (over the veto of President Johnson) for conferring the suffrage upon negroes in the district of Columbia (Jan. 7th and 8th, 1867).

tion was impossible. There was no other effectual and abiding check placed upon it but the will of the people, and to expect them to control it within theoretical limits was to place before them unlimited power and ask them not to use it.

It is a favourite boast with some Americans, although the idea by no means obtains universal assent among them, that the scheme of representation so laboriously prepared in the Federal and State Conventions confers upon the people the greatest advantages of which any arrangement of the elective franchise is capable. Whatever the cultivated classes may think, the masses believe that they have a more thorough and efficient representation in the national legislature than is known anywhere else in the world. And this belief is fortified by the authority of some of the most distinguished Americans. Webster says, the theory of representation "is admirably accommodated to our Constitution, better understood among us, and more familiarly and extensively practised, in the higher and in the lower departments of government, than it has been by any other people."[12] So, likewise, Chancellor Kent remarks—"The United States, in their improvements upon the exercise of the right of representation, may, as we apprehend, claim pre-eminence over all other governments, ancient and modern."[13] And Mr. Justice Story affirmed that every expedient which human ingenuity could

---

[12] Webster's Works, vol. i. p. 40. [13] 'Commentaries,' Lect. xi.

devise to make perfect the working of the machinery of government had been introduced "with singular skill, ingenuity, and wisdom, into the structure of the Constitution."[14] Notwithstanding this wisdom and skill, we have seen in our own day that the Legislative may be drawn into indecorous collision with the Executive, and that the action of the general government may for a time be paralysed by this unfortunate hostility. Year after year, too, there has been a growing conviction in the minds of the wealthy and cultivated classes that they are deprived of the influence which they ought rightfully to exercise in the affairs of the Republic, and that they have no protection against the encroachments of the majority. It is important to examine with some care into the circumstances which have served to bring into the light these faults and defects of the American theory of representation.

Mr. Madison laid it down as a fundamental axiom, that neither of the departments of the government "ought to possess, directly or indirectly, an overruling influence over the others in the administration of their respective powers." It is quite clear, however, that the tendency of events in recent years has been towards the accumulation of power in the hands of Congress to an extent which the authors of the Constitution never contemplated. In Madi-

---

[14] 'Commentaries,' vol. i. sect. 902. See also the 'Federalist,' Nos. 47-48.

son's day the first indications of this movement were apparent, and he acknowledges, with some regret, that the "legislative department is everywhere extending the sphere of its activity, and drawing all power into its impetuous vortex."[15] The construction of the government was such as to render this result not only probable, but unavoidable. Congress, proceeding immediately from the people, would naturally claim and exercise an overruling influence. It would only not seek to encroach upon the Executive and the Judiciary when those departments acted in harmony with it, or when it ceased to reflect perfectly the opinions of the people. When the Executive was its obedient instrument it would be satisfied with its position. But at other times it would refuse to be bound by "checks" and "balances" which were not found within itself—which it did not expressly make or accept. President Johnson, in his difficulties with Congress, laid much stress upon the opinions of eminent authorities that there was more to be feared from the tyranny of the Legislative than from the ambition of the Executive, for the latter power was confined within set limits, while the former was left almost without restraint.[16] He found himself stultified at every turn, and unable to give the slightest weight to his own opinions. And

---

[15] 'Federalist,' No. 48. See also the papers of Hamilton in the 'Federalist,' Nos. 72, 73.

[16] See the Veto of the Negro Suffrage Bill in the district of Columbia, 'Congressional Globe,' Jan. 8, 1867.

putting the situation in which he was actually placed as if it were merely a hypothetical situation, he wrote, "This would be a practical concentration of all power in the Congress of the United States—this, in the language of the author of the Declaration of Independence, would be 'precisely the definition of despotic government.'" But it is chiefly in critical periods, when the very safety of the nation appears to be endangered, or when some great principles precious in the eyes of the people seem about to be sacrificed, that Congress can obtain, and still less keep, this extraordinary monopoly of power. The convictions of the people must be deeply stirred before they will, by repeated elections, justify the virtual suppression of a most important department of the government. They must distrust the intentions of the Executive with regard to a policy of vital consequence to the Republic before they virtually depose him. In the time of Jackson the Executive made encroachments upon the Legislative which might well have excited alarm, but the true balance was not restored because the people did not interfere. They were content to let things take their course. But after the civil war, issues too momentous were at stake to permit of their remaining indifferent or passive spectators. They saw, or imagined that they saw, a determination on the part of the Executive to make another of those "compromises" which a disastrous experience had rendered inexpressibly hateful to them. The slavery question had been nursed by compromises until a peaceable solution of it became impossible, and between 1865-67 it seemed that the President had resolved to restore political power to the enemies of the government before it had well recovered from the shock which they had administered. Hence, Congress gradually found itself in the possession of an authority which it had never exercised before, and which the States that originally went into the Union would certainly never have consented to confer upon it. It did not assume anything more than the people then recognised to be in the Union gave it. It did not even, at the outset of the struggle, invade the province of the Executive. The President had it within his discretion to place a veto upon the acts of the Legistive, but the people had sent to that body a majority of two-thirds against him. He used the privilege which the Constitution gave him, and the people rendered it nugatory by the means which the Constitution had prescribed. To argue that under such circumstances Congress is a "despotism" is the same as to argue that the will of the people is a despotism; and that would be contrary to the principles of Republican governments, whatever the abstract truth may be. The citizens of other countries may see good reasons why they should not desire a rule based upon the will of varying and capricious majorities, but such a rule was voluntarily chosen, and is tenaciously clung to, by the people of America. They must abide by it, or change their form of government altogether.

The argument which was used in the Senate [17] against the President's assertions affecting Congress is unanswerable:—"The recent acts of Congress, those acts upon which the President and Congress separated, were submitted to the people, and after a very full canvass and a very able one, in which great numbers of speeches were made on both sides, and documents were circulated, the people, *who are the common masters of President and Congress,* decided in favour of Congress. Unless, therefore, there is an inherent danger from a republican government, resting solely upon the will of the people, there is no occasion for the warning of the President. Unless the judgment of one man is better than the combined judgment of a great majority, he should have respected their decision, and not continued a controversy in which our common constituency have decided that he was wrong."

This passage is not only a succinct commentary upon the powers of Congress, but it embodies an accurate description of the latest phase of Republicanism. It is manifest from their writings, and from the debates in the Convention of 1787, that the framers of the Constitution never expressly intended to give the supreme power to Congress. But this only shows that they failed to see whither republican principles would lead. They did not make sufficient allowance for the invincible force of popular opinion in a democracy. They thought to erect barriers between the will of the masses and the powers of government,

[17] By Senator Sherman, 'Congressional Globe,' Jan. 8th, 1867.

but these barriers fell down at a touch. It was only a qualified democracy which the originators of the American system wished to put into operation.[18] With the laws of the mother country, they wished to preserve some infusion of the spirit of its civil polity. But when everything is based upon the will of the people it is idle to think of controlling that will by urging reasons which appeal only to minds of a philosophic turn. In the United States the rule of the masses has constantly grown stronger, and it must continue to grow, and therefore it would be well for themselves if they chose as the instruments of their work men of high integrity and honour, and thus made good their boast that they enjoy the best representative system known to mankind.

It is upon this latter point that so great a difference of opinion exists among Americans who are the most deeply attached to their country and its institutions. It is seen by them to be very questionable whether Congress has not partially failed both as a representative and a deliberative body. No one can affirm that either property or intellect is adequately represented. Webster thought that political power would naturally and inevitably pass into the hands which held the property,[19] but it is found in

---

[18] Madison disclaims the title "Democracy," and expresses his preference for the word "Republicanism." 'Federalist,' No. 10.

[19] Speech on "Basis of the Senate."—Works,. iii. p. 15. The same opinion was expressed on many occasions in the Philadelphia Convention of 1787. See Elliot's 'Debates.'

practice that the bulk of the community, which is poor or of but moderate means, choose men of their own class to represent them, and politicians find it to their advantage to study the wishes of this class rather than of any other. Even in journals of extreme republican principles it is not uncommon to find this fact admitted and deplored. "Nobody," remarked one such writer, "who has paid much attention to our political discussions of late years, both in and out of Congress, can have avoided being struck by the general tendency to exalt and glorify the poor, apparently for the simple reason that they are poor, and in a corresponding degree to depreciate 'the rich;' and, singularly enough, the standard of wealth seems to be, in political phraseology, every year sinking lower and lower."[20] In large cities men of property or culture frequently refrain from exercising their right of suffrage, either because they consider the candidates unfit to go into Congress, or because they know that their votes would be thrown away. This is a great evil, but one of a still more serious character exists in the absence of a proportionate representation of the minority in the United States. This has been found a defect which it has defied the ingenuity of statesmen to remove in other constitutional countries, but there are peculiar circumstances arising out of party government in America which render it there unusually mischievous. As we

[20] 'North American Review,' July, 1865.

shall see hereafter, it is almost impossible for a man of independent opinions to obtain a seat in Congress. He must be "endorsed" by a party, and slavishly adopt all the views of that party, or it is useless for him to contest an election. Should any accepted member exhibit an opinion of his own in opposition to the general party, he is practically driven out of its ranks, he is assailed on all sides with a virulence and unscrupulousness unknown elsewhere, he inevitably fails to receive a future nomination, and thus he loses the next election. Within the walls of the Legislature every voice is raised against him, and outside he has to confront the unprincipled assaults of the combined agents of a faction. Few public men in America can long contend in so unequal a struggle. Thus the power of Congress is securely concentrated in the hands of the leaders of the dominant party of the hour, who may be so actuated by personal ambition, or other unworthy motives, as to render them altogether unsafe guides for the nation. The discussions of this conclave are carried on in secret, and the mockery of a deliberative assembly is made complete by the systematic refusal to allow of full debate upon measures of the most momentous description. They are decided upon in private caucus, for reasons which the public are not allowed to know; and when they are brought forward in the Legislature, by a form of the House of Representatives known as the "previous question," which the adherents of the governing party are almost always numerous enough to enforce, discussion is absolutely prevented. Sometimes no one is allowed to say a word. The minority is not admitted to the caucus, and in the House a gag is placed upon their mouths. When the Civil Rights Bill was passed over the President's veto in April, 1866, several independent members begged hard for permission to discuss it, or at least to explain their reasons for the vote they intended to give. It was refused, and there was a general cry in the House "Give an hour!" but the leaders were inexorable, and the resolution was pressed to a division in less than ten minutes after it had been sent to the Speaker. The same practice was afterwards adopted, and with uniform success. It is true that in the Senate there is no power to forbid discussion, but one branch of the Legislative, and that the popular branch, submits quietly to a tyranny which is destructive of the true principles of a legislative assembly, and a betrayal of the trust confided to it by the people.

Nearly all questions of domestic policy are discussed in Congress from the standpoint of local interests. If the subject of protection for commerce and manufactures is before the assembly, each member considers it as it affects his own constituents, and there is no one to represent the general interests of the nation. Those members alone speak who have local objects to promote;[21] the majority are ignorant

[21] A member of Congress must almost always be a resident in the district which he represents.

of the subject, and the two years for which they are elected is too short a time to enable them to acquaint themselves properly with it, or to adopt fixed and settled principles. In all questions which arise it is the recognised system for members to ascertain what their constituents wish, not to study what would be best for the welfare of the whole Republic. An English member of Parliament is supposed to be alive to the fact that there is a large class besides his constituency whom it is his duty to represent. There are occasions when he feels it incumbent upon him to represent that class, rather than, or even against, his own constituency. This standard of public honour is rarely indeed exhibited in America. The member of Congress surrenders all his opinions to his constituents. He says what they command him to say, no more and no less. He is the slave of his supporters and of his party. Constantly one may hear it said in the House of Representatives, "I believe this measure to be unwise, but my constituents want it and they must have it. What is the use of going against them?"[22] Few men of eminent ability will accept a seat in Congress upon such terms, and hence the lament is general that the tone of Congress is constantly declining. Men of character and talents will not barter away their independence of judgment and their matured convictions for the

---

[22] Theoretically, the member of Congress is supposed to represent the nation (see Story's 'Commentaries,' sect. 587), but in practice the system undoubtedly prevails which is described in the text.

doubtful honour of becoming the mouthpiece of a tyrannical faction for a period of two years. The best men of business, the men of wealth and leisure, the cultivated classes, cannot as a rule be prevailed upon to put themselves forward as candidates for Congress. The natural operation of the suffrage is partly the cause of this, but it must also be referred to the fact that political life in America is not usually an object of ambition with the well-informed classes. The independent member of Congress is not always allowed to state his opinions. If another Webster or Clay appeared in the House of Representatives, he would probably be silenced by a demand for the previous question, or some other device of the majority to silence discussion. In the Reform debates of 1865-67 in the English Parliament, speeches of commanding power and eloquence were occasionally delivered against the popular side. In a similar condition of public feeling in the United States there is scarcely any public man of position who would dare to exercise this freedom of thought and opinion. There he must go with the tide or be washed away. And hence the remark made by an English public writer, during the despotism of Congress in 1866, was profoundly true and just—"It may be pronounced an absolute impossibility that a man like the late Sir George Cornewall Lewis, capable of seeing two sides of a question, should be returned to Congress." Or, what is the same thing, if he were returned it would be because his constituents had not detected his impartial faculty, and as soon as they did perceive it they would turn him out.

What we find represented and advocated in Congress are sectional differences rather than broad and comprehensive principles based upon considerations of the general good of the people.[23] This is of less consequence in America than it would be in England, since the States by their own laws can provide for the social well-being of their inhabitants. They can regulate their own affairs, and place the means of education within the reach of all. Except, therefore, when a question arises which affects all the States, and which no single State, or number of States less than the whole, can control, it is not important that a deputy should do more than protect the interests

---

[23] In the New York Convention which assembled to ratify the Constitution Mr. Hamilton said,—"In my experience of public affairs I have constantly remarked, in the conduct of members of Congress, a strong and uniform attachment to the interests of their own State. These interests have, on many occasions, been adhered to with an undue and illiberal pertinacity, and have too often been preferred to the interests of the Union. This attachment has given birth to an unaccommodating spirit of party which has frequently embarrassed the best measures."—(Elliot's 'Débates,' ii. 266.) Hamilton was, in some respects, a man of greater sagacity and foresight than almost any of his contemporaries. Few besides himself acknowledged that there was anything to be regretted in the attachment of a member to his locality regardless of the interest of the Republic. Talleyrand told Mr. Martin Van Buren that "he regarded Hamilton as the ablest man he became acquainted with in America—he was not sure that he might not add without injustice, or that he had known in Europe."—(See Van Buren's 'Political Parties,' p. 124.)

of his own constituency. But when a crisis does arise which requires the united action of all the members, they have localities so much in mind and the welfare of the community so little, that agreement can only be arrived at by that device which has received the humourous name of "log-rolling." One member votes for his friend's proposition to-day upon the understanding that his friend will return the civility to-morrow. But as the idea of a "nation" grows upon the people sectional affairs will be more and more confined to State Legislatures. And as a natural consequence, power will accumulate in the hands of Congress, and the States must sacrifice some portion of their former functions in order that they may be welded together in a solid body, and thus reveal an unbroken front to the rest of the world.

CHAPTER VI.

THE JUDICIARY.

THE absence of a well-organised judicial power in the old Confederation was one of its most obvious defects. There was no supreme tribunal to which questions arising between States, or affecting the construction of treaties, could be referred. Each State interpreted as it pleased a compact which assumed to be binding upon all. The derangement of public affairs which such a want of system produced may easily be imagined. There was no certainty that an arrangement entered into between the States would be honourably observed, because, when any of the parties to it became dissatisfied, it was easy to put a new construction upon the agreement, and there was no recognised authority by which the dispute could be adjusted. This deficiency must have been a constant source of inconvenience and embarrassment to each of the members in turn. "The treaties of the United States," said Hamilton, "under the present Constitution are liable to the infraction of thirteen different Legislatures, and as many different courts of final jurisdiction, acting under the authority of those Legislatures."[1] The result was that nothing was settled—nothing secured. A covenant was only binding so long as every State chose to acknowledge its validity.

To remedy these inconveniences a Supreme Court was established by the Constitution, and authority was given to Congress to create inferior courts from time to time as occasion demanded.[2] In each State there exist courts intrusted with the administration of the local, or State, laws, and a Supreme Court is established over all. The State tribunals decide a cause in the first instance, and if it involves a question which comes within the province of the Federal Supreme Court it may be carried there upon appeal. The system works in a circle—the State Courts, the Supreme Court of the State to decide appeals, and the Federal Supreme Court, which is clad with the exclusive authority to pronounce final judgment on all questions affecting the Constitution, the construction of laws, the interpretation of treaties, and other subjects expressly designated in the Constitution itself. In the appointment of the State judges the principle of conferring office for a short period only is adopted, and thus the control of the Bench has practically fallen into the hands of the majority. In vain the thoughtful class of Americans have warned their countrymen against the mischiefs which must accrue from this degradation of the judicial office.

---

[1] 'Federalist,' No. 22.

[2] Art. III. sec. 1.

The judges, it is contended, should be the servants of the people, and remain subject to their supervision and control. In the state of New York the election of judges by universal suffrage has created a scandal which is keenly felt by the nation. With some honourable exceptions, the judges in the State, but especially in the city, are notoriously corrupt or incapable, and owe their election to the very class against which the protection of the law is most needed by peaceable citizens. The most shameful offences are constantly committed by men placed upon the Bench by the popular vote. They listen privately to one or other of the suitors in a case which is afterwards to be brought before them, and openly take bribes for their decisions. It was well known that one judge received ten thousand dollars for giving judgment in a case, and he still remained upon the Bench. Their language is sometimes coarse and profane to the last degree. "If," remarks an American writer, "we were to relate half the rumours which are afloat, and which are fully credited, too, by the most intelligent and discreet members of the bar, we should draw a picture as appalling as anything to be found in the books of the prophets Amos and Micah."[3]

---

[3] See the 'North American Review,' for July, 1867 (pp. 148-176), where any one interested in this subject may find a story of corruption unparalleled in the modern judicial annals of any country. The statements made by the writer, although they so seriously affected the character of many judges, were never contradicted in New

Since each State has the power to make laws for itself, it follows that there is no uniformity in the measures adopted for the punishment of crime or the regulation of society. Take, for instance, the law relating to divorce. In some States there must not only be a judicial investigation and decision, but the assent of two-thirds of each branch of the Legislature is necessary to make a decree lawful. In South Carolina no divorce has ever been granted, "so strict and scrupulous," as Mr. Justice Kent says has been the policy of the State in relation to marriage. Some of the newer States go to the other extreme. In Kentucky, if the wife leaves her husband for one year a divorce is granted, and it frequently happens that married persons wishing to be separated go to that State and live apart by mutual agreement, and so obtain a divorce upon easy terms. In Indiana and Missouri abandonment by either party for two years is a sufficient ground for divorce, and the extraordinary discretion is also allowed to the court of granting a divorce upon any pretext which it may deem "reasonable and proper." In Tennessee the wilful absence of husband or wife for two years secures the divorce. In the laws of New Hampshire there is the curious provision that if the husband joins the society known as "the Shakers," and remains in it for three years, his wife can obtain judicial separation. In Ohio habitual

York. Every one admitted the facts, but many deprecated their publication, upon the ground that it "could do no good."

drunkenness for three years is held to be sufficient cause for granting a decree, and the same law exists in Maine. But Kentucky is the most lax in her marriage laws. Besides the ground of divorce already stated, she provides that divorce may be allowed if the jury find "that either party has unnecessarily exposed, in a public paper, the other to public notoriety and reproach for alleged abandonment," or "by other unnecessary and cruel conduct endeavoured to disgrace the same." These laws were made in 1850. In some of the States the proportion of divorces to marriages is said to reach thirty per cent.

The laws relating to the inheritance or transfer of land vary in a similar manner, and it has been stated by an American jurist that there is no general law of descents in the country. To cite a few examples of this diversity: in many of the States it is the law that, "if the owner of lands dies without lawful descendants, leaving parents, the inheritance shall ascend to them."[4] In Vermont the widow, there being no children, takes half the estate, and the father of the deceased the other half. In Massachusetts and Arkansas the estate devolves to the father. In Louisiana a moiety of the estate of an intestate, in default of issue, goes to the father and mother, and the remainder to the brothers and sisters and their descendants. Most of the other

[4] Kent, p. 431.

States have adopted the principle of giving parents the right of succession to the property of their children dying intestate. Estates tail existed in America until the Revolution, but they were gradually abolished by the different States, and converted into fees simple. In New York, as Kent informs us, "the power of protracting the period of alienation has been restricted to two successive estates for life, limited to the lives of two persons in being at the creation of the estate."[5]

The composition of the Federal Judiciary was a labour of great anxiety to the Convention of 1787, and to the subsequent State Conventions. Should the judicial power be merged in the Legislature or be left distinct? Should the Judiciary be privileged to annul laws? How should the judges be appointed? These and many other questions were discussed with great patience and ability, until it seemed that every possible ramification of the subject had been thoroughly explored. Among other propositions brought forward there was one to place the power of appointing judges in the Legislature. This was earnestly opposed by several members, on the ground that it would give rise to intrigue and partiality. One member reminded the Convention that a principal reason for insisting on unity in the Executive "was that officers might be appointed by a single responsible person."[6] Mr. Madison suggested as a

---

[5] Kent, p. 17.

[6] Madison's 'Reports,' p. 155.

compromise that the appointing power should rest with the Senate, and for some time the Convention remained undecided in their choice between the Executive and the Senate. Eventually it was resolved that the appointments should be made by the President, subject to the approval and confirmation of the Senate. In this state the law still remains, and when judges are once appointed they remain in office during good behaviour; that is, they can be removed only by impeachment. But, as has been described with reference to New York, the State courts are regulated according to the will of the people. In two States the judges, even of the Supreme Courts, are annually elected by ballot; in most others the office is given for a limited period only.[7] The Federal Supreme Court consists of a Chief Justice and eight associate judges, five of whom form a quorum. It meets simultaneously with the regular Session of Congress, on the first Monday in every December, and holds its sittings at Washington. One of the judges, conjointly with a district judge, holds two courts a year in each of the nine circuits into which the country is divided, and these are called Circuit Courts.[8] In a strictly judicial capacity the State courts are thrown into more direct connexion with the social life of the people than the Supreme Court, which only occupies itself with the highest range of questions.

[7] See Kent's 'Commentaries,' i., *note* to p. 309.
[8] Ibid. Lect. xiv.

The third department of the government was designed to act as a check or counterpoise to the other two. The maintenance of the Constitution, and the protection of all lawful rights, were objects confined to the Judiciary, and it was thought that it was armed with ample powers to make its authority respected, and to guard against encroachment upon its functions. On this point it is not possible that there can be a difference of opinion. The words of the authorities, early and late, are not to be misunderstood. The *Federalist* took pains to point out the importance of preserving "the complete independence of the courts of justice."[9] The Convention was unanimously of this view, and Washington declared that the Judiciary was the chief pillar on which the national government must rest.[10] "I cannot," says Chancellor Kent, "conceive of anything more grand and imposing in the whole administration of human justice than the spectacle of the Supreme Court sitting in solemn judgment upon the conflicting claims of the national and State sovereignties, and tranquillising all jealous and angry passions, and binding together this great confederacy of States in peace and harmony, by the ability, the moderation, and the equity of its decisions."[11] And concerning the State courts he remarks, "The true interests and the permanent freedom of this country

[9] No. 78.
[10] Sparks' 'Writings of Washington,' vol. x., pp. 35, 86.
[11] 'Commentaries,' i. p. 482. (Lect. xix.)

require that the jurisprudence of the individual States should be cultivated, cherished, and exalted, and the dignity and reputation of the State authorities sustained with becoming pride."[12]

These opinions, although of a nature to recommend themselves to every generation, seem to be now abandoned. Congress has swept away by its own fiat the whole Judiciary system of ten States, and thus established a precedent which must produce incalculable mischief hereafter. The most eminent lawyers of the day protested against this rash measure, but no one listened to them. Congress had ordered it, and the people do not appear to have given their attention to it sufficiently to discern its extreme importance. The act was the more to be deplored because there was no necessity for it. The general government could have been securely protected against treason and traitors without the abolition of all local courts of justice in disaffected States. The Federal Judiciary itself was unable to stand before the pressure of the Legislative. It could not be greater than the people. It could not prevent laws being passed; and although it might declare those laws to be unconstitutional, it had no power to enforce its decrees. The people, if they were inclined to disregard the Constitution, could not be restrained by any action of the Supreme Court. Prior even to the civil war, but repeatedly since, the decisions

[12] Ibid. p. 483. See also Story, 'Commentaries,' Book III. chapter iv.

of the court upon constitutional questions have produced no effect whatever on either Congress or the people. The Dred Scott decision was technically law until slavery was abolished by a constitutional amendment, but as a general rule it was disregarded. In 1866 the Supreme Court decided that military tribunals were unlawful,[13] and the government of the South was afterwards made one great military tribunal, the Generals in command of the States being empowered to remove judges and all civil officers at their pleasure. In another case brought before the Supreme Court it was decided that the application of a test oath of the State of Missouri was in contravention of the clause in the Constitution, which provides "that no State shall pass any bill of attainder" or "*ex post facto* law;" and yet test oaths, of a retrospective and most rigorous character, were afterwards applied to all persons who presented themselves at the polls in the Southern States. What could the Supreme Court do but stand helplessly on one side and look on at the miscarriage of its decisions? Until a "case" was brought before it there was no opportunity even to make its voice heard, and after that it had no means of exacting obedience. Like all other institutions, it stood at the mercy of the majority. It had no resources to draw upon unless the people came resolutely to its support, and sent representatives to Congress who were

---

[13] Case, *ex parte* Lambdin *v.* Milligan *et al.*

pledged to restore it to its theoretical position in the Government. Mr. Justice Story was strongly of opinion that the Supreme Court was not bound to observe the rescripts of the majority, and that the common sense of the people would always lead them to prevent the Legislature from tampering with the Constitution. Would not a contrary course, he asked, "make the Constitution an instrument of flexible and changeable interpretation, and not a settled form of government with fixed limitations? Would it not become, instead of a supreme law for ourselves and our posterity, a mere oracle of the powers of the rulers of the day, to which implicit homage is to be paid, and speaking at different times the most opposite commands, and in the most ambiguous voices?"[14] It would not be possible to borrow language which described with greater accuracy and fidelity the Constitution and the Judiciary as they are. Story thought he was picturing a state of things which could never be witnessed in his country, whereas he but anticipated the inevitable changes which were impending over the method of government he was so anxious to defend.

The falsification of all statements and speculations concerning the Judiciary was precipitated by the civil war, and this consideration renders some of M. de Tocqueville's assertions at least comprehensible. The judges, he declares, are invested with "immense

---

[14] 'Commentaries,' ii. p. 462.

political power." "The Americans have acknowledged the right of the judges to found their decisions on the Constitution rather than on the laws. In other words, they have not permitted them to apply such laws as may appear to them to be unconstitutional."[15] So far from this being the case, we find that the people practically compel the Supreme Court to apply laws which it has pronounced unconstitutional. The Legislature first passes such laws, the people support the Legislature, and the Government is obliged to see that the laws are carried into execution. The Supreme Court simply sits upon the Bench uttering protests which no one heeds, while the unconstitutional measures are being enforced out of doors. M. de Tocqueville affirms that "not a party, not so much as an individual, is found to contest" the authority which he ascribes to the Supreme Court. This is one of the positive statements which startle and confound those who have been accustomed to place dependence on M. de Tocqueville's work. The strong party in the United States has always been opposed to the Judiciary, and since the rebellion the ruling party has systematically repudiated all the claims of the Supreme Court. They even threatened to "revolutionise" it if it continued refractory and obstinate—that is, if it adhered to the principles laid down for its guidance in the Constitution. And they might at any time fulfil this

[15] Vol. i chapter vi. p. 125. (Tome i. p. 166.)

menace by increasing the number of judges, and then refusing to confirm the appointment of any but those of their own opinions. The controlling and arresting force which De Tocqueville detected in the construction of the Supreme Court, was a fiction which he invented or imagined to perfect the general harmony of his theory. "The power," he remarks, "vested in the American Courts of Justice, of pronouncing a statute to be unconstitutional, forms one of the most powerful barriers which has ever been devised against the tyranny of political assemblies."[16] He did not see that there was nothing behind the barrier to support it, and that consequently it was doomed to disappear before a breath of popular will. It did not need the extraordinary acuteness with which M. de Tocqueville has been credited to perceive that the "tyranny of a political assembly" might easily be irresistible when exercised against a power which was nothing in itself, and which derived all its vitality from the concurrence of that very assembly. While the Judiciary was unopposed it was supreme; when it was reduced to act on the defensive all its power and majesty disappeared.

"The Supreme Court of the United States," observes M. de Tocqueville in another portion of his work, "is the sole tribunal of the nation." He forgot that its favourite tribunal is *itself*. Through the Legislature the people make known their wishes,

---

[16] Vol. I. chap. vi. pp. 129-30. (Tome i. p. 172.)

and to those wishes the Executive and Judiciary, being entirely unarmed, must always succumb. "The very existence of the Union," says M. de Tocqueville, "is vested in the hands of the seven Federal judges." What could they do for the Union when it was assailed by the South? "The Executive," he further states, "appeals to them (the judges) for assistance against the encroachments of the Legislative."[17] And when it does—as it did between 1865 and 1867—what assistance can the judges render? They may decide that the Executive is right, but, if the nation say that he is wrong, which will be likely to have its own way?—the people who have control over the physical arm, or the Executive who is helpless whenever he alienates from his side the governing party? De Tocqueville did indeed foresee that circumstances might arise which would overset his theories. He admitted that the judges "would be impotent against popular neglect or contempt of the law." But when he allowed that such an event might happen he contradicted every statement which he had advanced, and every inference which he had drawn, with respect to the place in the government of the Supreme Court. He reasoned from abstract principles, or from his own ideal of the American Republic, and these were constantly in conflict with his experience.

The momentous crisis of the last few years, which

---

17 Vol. i. p. 191. (Tome i. p. 252).

produced so many vital changes in the structure of the government, left the Judiciary stripped of its most precious prerogatives. If Chancellor Kent were living to revise his lectures, he would feel himself constrained to omit that passage in which he says,—"There can be no doubt upon the point with us, that every act of the legislative power, contrary to the true interest and meaning of the Constitution, is absolutely null and void."[18] No one pretended that the measures passed by Congress after the South laid down its arms were in accordance even with the spirit of the Constitution, while almost all acknowledged that they openly violated its letter. The party which introduced those measures, justified them upon the ground that an emergency had arisen which was sufficient to call a power into existence greater than that of the Constitution. Congress prescribed the terms of suffrage for all the Southern States, although the Constitution is express in declaring that this was a question which for all future time every State should be left to determine for itself. It took away from the States the power of appointing their own civil officers, and excluded the bulk of the inhabitants entirely from the suffrage. It enfranchised the blacks, and disfranchised the whites. These and many similar acts were defended on the ground of necessity or expediency, or upon the plea that the insurgent States had forfeited their

---

[18] 'Commentaries,' Part III. Lect. xx, p. 486, vol. i.

former rights under the Union; but the Constitution gave no warrant for such an exercise of legislative responsibility. Had its dictates been heeded, it would have placed, as it was intended to do, a restraint upon that power which was aiming to destroy States, whose inviolability had been guaranteed by the most solemn compact ever entered into between men. Had the Supreme Court been moved, it must have pronounced judgment on these laws according to the teaching of the Constitution alone; it would have declared them null and void, and beyond this it could do nothing. Whenever it decided against a popular measure it discredited itself by an impotent display of authority. Any one who examines closely into the history of the war and of subsequent events, will be astonished at the small and despised part which the Supreme Court, the intended source of the reserved power of the Republic, played throughout. The founders of the Constitution would have predicated that it would have acted as the great peacemaker after the war —allaying animosities and extinguishing jealousies, tempering the excesses of the victorious, and softening the humiliations of the vanquished party. This was the province it would have fulfilled had it been true to the theory of its construction, or had it realised the expectations of later writers. Chancellor Kent looked to the Supreme Court, "venerable by its gravity, its dignity, and its wisdom," as an unfailing safeguard against the tyranny of majorities, and the probable destruction of free institutions. "If there was no check," he says, "upon the tyranny of legislative majorities, the prospect before us would be gloomy in the extreme." These are remarkable words, both from the weight of the authority from which they proceed, and from the fact that we must now read them in the nature of a prediction. The possibility imagined by Chancellor Kent is the reality of to-day, and must remain the unalterable condition of the political system. There is no check upon the Legislative majority. Come what may, it is supreme. It bends the Executive—it defies or ignores the Judiciary. Whether the consequences be good or evil, the rule of the majority must henceforth be a tyranny. Minorities have no rights except such as are conceded to them by the majority.[19]

It cannot be too often repeated that this degradation of the Federal Judiciary was never contemplated by the founders of the Constitution. It was expected that the people would at all times be ready to bow to its decisions, and no provision was made, or could have been made, for such an event as their denying or repudiating its authority. Mr. Ellsworth, after-

---

[19] Chancellor Kent appears to have had a foreboding of this result. "The equal rights of a minor party," he says, in a note to his 20th Lecture (vol. i. p. 488), "are disregarded in the animated competitions for power; and if it were not for the checks and barriers to which I have alluded, they would fall a sacrifice to the passions of fierce and vindictive majorities." The danger which he dreaded is actually before his country, but, whether it is so fatal as he supposed it, time alone can decide.

wards Chief-Justice, well put this point in the Convention of Connecticut. "If the United States go beyond their powers; if they make a law, which the Constitution does not authorize, it is void; and the judicial power, the national judges, who, to secure their impartiality, are to be made independent, will declare it void." "Still, however," he added, "if the United States and the individual States will quarrel—if they want to fight, they may do it, and no frame of government can possibly prevent it."[20] And so, too, Chief-Justice Marshall observed that, "whenever hostility to the existing system shall become universal, it will also be irresistible. The people made the Constitution, and the people can unmake it. It is the creature of their will, and lives only by their will."

It is impossible to foretell the ultimate consequences of the prostration of the Supreme Court. In quiet times, and when no issue which divides the nation is being contested, the decisions of the Court may still be regarded as binding upon all; but it is evident that the Legislature, when supported by a majority, can always go on making laws which are manifestly and avowedly not in agreement with the Constitution, and that the Supreme Court has no power to prevent these enactments from being put in force against the minority. Its jurisdiction may be questioned, and its judgments set at nought.

---

[20] Story, 'Commentaries" p. 267 (3rd ed. *note*), Book iii. c. iv.

There will then arise that state of things which Mr. Justice Story described as a day of evil never likely to be witnessed in the United States:—"The people may, if they please, submit all power to their rulers for the time being; but then the government should receive its true appellation and character. It would be a government of tyrants, elective, it is true, but still tyrants; and it would become the more fierce, vindictive, and sanguinary because it would perpetually generate factions in its own bosom, who could succeed only by the ruin of their enemies. . . . . It would be as corrupt as it would be dangerous. It would form another model of that profligate and bloody democracy, which, at one time, in the French Revolution, darkened by its deeds the fortunes of France, and left to mankind the appalling lesson, that virtue and religion, genius and learning, the authority of wisdom and the appeals of innocence, are unheard and unfelt in the frenzy of popular excitement; and that the worst crimes may be sanctioned, and the most desolating principles inculcated, under the banners and in the name of liberty."[21] This picture is a gloomy one, and every American would shrink back from the thought that there is a possibility it may be realized some day in his own land. But such catastrophes are always unforeseen. No nation ever believed that the violent convulsions which they find recorded in history they also are

[21] 'Commentaries,' ii. p. 468, sect. 1621.

destined to undergo. They wonder at the blindness and folly of the people who thus suffered, while at the same time they may be pursuing a course which must end in precisely the same results. Already the Americans are accustomed to see vast social and political changes carried out without reference to that "collected will" of which Webster speaks. The idea, so precious to the constructors of the government, that there should be one settled law, placed above the reach of time or change, by which all questions relating to the functions of any department of the government might be judged, has proved a dream. Laws will be made for the day. "A community," says a distinguished jurist, "which never hesitated to relax rules of written law whenever they stood in the way of an ideally perfect decision on the facts of particular cases, would only, if it bequeathed any body of judicial principles to posterity, bequeath one consisting of the ideas of right and wrong which happened to be prevalent at the time."[22] It was wise in the Americans to improve their Constitution. But to undermine the tribunal which must be the expounder of that Constitution was an act of recklessness which is likely to be profoundly deplored hereafter by all classes of the people.

---

[22] Maine's 'Ancient Law,' chapter iv.

CHAPTER VII.

UNIVERSAL SUFFRAGE.

THE Federal Constitution left to the States in the Union the power which they originally possessed of determining for themselves the qualifications of electors, with the single condition that the electors for members of the House of Representatives "shall have the qualifications requisite for electors of the most numerous branch of the State Legislature."[1] Thus, uniformity is not found in the electoral system of the United States, and it cannot be strictly said that universal suffrage exists there. The laws of nearly all the States vary upon this important subject, and until very recently Congress had not assumed the right to dictate to any State the terms upon which it should admit its citizens to the franchise. But after the fall of the Southern Confederacy it decided that by right of conquest it could justly deprive the insurgent States of their "equal right of representation" until they consented to allow

[1] Constitution, art. i. sect. 2.

negroes to vote, and in 1867 the same Congress advanced a step farther than this, and refused to admit into the Union two Territories as States unless they changed the organic law of their Constitutions so that it should not exclude negroes from the suffrage. This measure was not carried without protests and arguments from many members, who maintained that it was a proceeding utterly without precedent and warrant in Congress to fetter the States in their action upon an essential part of their internal policy, with which the Constitution inferentially forbade interference. But other members did not hesitate to affirm that Congress not only had the right to exclude new States, until they complied with any conditions it thought proper to impose, but that it ought also to insist upon States already in the Union modifying their Constitutions so that the emancipated race might be on an equality at the polls with the white citizen. "Pennsylvania," said one of the representatives of that State, "has not at this moment a Republican form of government, and I wish that Congress would compel it to organise one."[2] And although these views were warmly opposed, still both houses of Congress refused by a large majority to admit Nebraska and Colorado as States until they had changed the electoral qualifications upon which they had fixed, and abolished distinction on the ground of race or colour.

---

[2] See the debate in the House of Representatives, Jan. 15, 1867.

The older States had, of course, decided upon the qualifications of electors long before the troubles of the civil war. Some of them made it conditional that before a citizen could vote he must have paid a State or county tax; in others a certain period of residence was prescribed; in Illinois, Iowa, and other Western States, any person may vote, whether naturalised or not, if he has lived six months in a "fixed permanent residence." In Maine a three months' residence is the only qualification. In Pennsylvania he must have paid a tax within two years, and lived one year in the State and ten days in the district. In four States a property qualification is exacted. In the mode of voting the practice is not uniform; in some States it is *viva voce*, in others by ballot.[3] And the custom of open voting is commended by some American publicists of high authority in preference to the ballot, which is chiefly extolled in countries where it has not yet been introduced, and where the corruption to which it gives rise is not realised or understood. Thus Mr. Justice Story writes—"Intrigue and combination are more commonly found connected with secret sessions than with public debates; with the working of the ballot-box than with the manliness of *viva voce* votes. At least it may be questioned if the vote by ballot has, in the opinion of a majority of the American people, obtained any preference over *viva voce* voting, even

[3] See 'The Constitution of the United States' (New York, 1857), and also Kent's 'Commentaries,' i. pp. 231-34, *note*.

at elections."[4] It will presently be shown that the effect of the ballot is not to prevent bribery, but merely to enable corrupt electors to receive money from each of the contestants, and to be shielded from all risk of discovery. Undoubtedly a man may keep his vote secret if he have any special object to accomplish thereby, but it is not an aim with men of principle to disguise their opinions. Their views are known, or may be known to any one who takes an interest in them, beforehand. The only advantage of the ballot is that it prevents the noise and confusion which often prevail in the *viva voce* mode of election. The voter drops his ticket quietly into a glass globe, which is kept securely locked, and a much larger number of votes can be registered in the same space of time by this arrangement, than by the process of open voting.

---

[4] Story's 'Commentaries,' i. sect. 841. American politicians are often found intensely hostile to the ballot. On the 14th of March, 1867, in the course of a debate in the Senate upon a reconstruction bill for the South, a Radical senator (Mr. Trumbull) said—"I want to see every man an independent voter, not sneaking to the polls and hiding his expression in a secret ballot. Sir, it is by secret ballots and secret systems of other kinds that liberty has been trodden down everywhere. I have no such opinion of my fellow-countrymen, I have no such opinion of the masses of the people of this country, as to suppose that they dare not tell out how they vote." Another senator (Mr. Buckalew) said that the advantages of the vote by ballot had been very much over-estimated, particularly abroad—'It leads to nothing but deception; and deception which can only be practised by the cunning, and which cannot be and is not practised by the simple, for whose protection the system was originally established."—(See the 'Daily Congressional Globe' of March 15th, 1867.)

The mode of exercising the franchise seems at first sight to be involved and complicated, but it is in reality perfectly clear and simple. In State elections the people elect the members of the House, and the Legislature ballots for Senators. The Legislature of each State chooses the Senators to represent it in the Federal Congress; but the people at large vote directly at the polls for members of the House of Representatives. In Congress the Senate is intended to represent *States;* the House of Representatives, the *people.* It is important that the general system should be thoroughly understood, and it is necessary that each part of it should be examined in detail, in order that it may be rightly seen into what hands political power actually falls. Let us first consider the mode of electing the President of the United States.

The founders of the government earnestly desired to break the direct action of the people in the choice of President. It was provided that the people of a State should not vote for their chief magistrate, but that they should, either directly or through their State Legislatures, select a number of persons, equal to the number of representatives to which they were entitled in Congress, and that these persons, called "Electors," should meet on a given day, and cast their votes for the President. The express design was that the Electors should be left free to exercise their own independent judgment and will. They would, it was thought, weigh carefully the merits of each candidate, and be less liable to the influences of party passion or feeling than the mass of the people. They would discharge their important trust in a calm and judicial spirit, and, since no pay or emoluments were attached to their duties, they would do what was required of them without fear or favour. The four electors from Rhode Island, equal to her two Representatives and two Senators, and the thirty-four electors from New York, equal to her thirty-two Representatives and two Senators,[5] would meet in their respective States, and form an opinion of their own with regard to the candidates before them, and would not be afraid of voting in accordance with that opinion. This is the constitutional theory of a Presidential Election. Upon this all the recognised authorities are agreed, and, as the practice is altogether opposed to the theory, it is well to consider the words of two or three of these authorities. Hamilton evidently thought that an effectual barrier against the direct force of the people in the choice of President had been provided. "The choice of several," he says, "to form an intermediate body of electors, will be much less apt to convulse the community with any extraordinary or violent movements, than the choice of *one*, who was himself to be the final object of the public wishes."[6] In the same spirit Chancellor Kent tells us that the Constitution "has not thought it safe or prudent to refer

[5] These are the numbers at the present time, not, of course, at the outset of the government.

[6] 'Federalist,' No. 68.

the election of a President directly and immediately to the people,"[7] because, as he goes on to explain, a "popular election might have led to a violent contest, and tried the experiment on too extended a scale for the public virtue, tranquillity, and happiness."[8] All the evils incidental to a popular appeal had, he thought, been avoided by this scheme of a special electoral body. The Electors would be free from all temptations to bias or corruption. Mr. Justice Story adopts precisely the same line of argument, but admits that the system contemplated by the founders of the Constitution has been utterly departed from.[9]

In this feature of their plan, as in so many others, the framers of the Constitution were misled by their confidence in artificial checks and safeguards. They miscalculated the effect of placing the moving springs of government in the hands of the masses. They thought that the people would be permanently satisfied with something short of the whole, and either did not perceive the tendency of popular government to end in unbridled indulgence of the will of mere numbers, or thought the evil too remote to occasion anxiety. The results of this error of judgment are apparent in every detail of the civil polity. The corruption and immorality incidental to a great personal contest like that of a Presidental election were deemed to be securely guarded against, whereas they are now established with the force and sanction of custom in

7 'Commentaries,' Lect. xiii. sect. 275. 8 Ibid. sect. 279.
9 Story's 'Commentaries,' vol. ii sect. 1457 and 1463.

every part of the Union. The ingenious apparatus for filtering public opinion has been discarded. The Executive of the United States is in fact elected by a popular vote, but no national convulsion ordinarily follows the retiring or brings in the succeeding President. On a certain day the people go to the polls to choose Electors. The names of the candidates are printed on tickets, at the head of which is the name of the Presidential candidate whom they are pledged to support. When the citizen votes this ticket, he in effect votes directly for the man he desires to see President, for the Electors afterwards fulfil a purely delegated function—they go through a form required by the Constitution, but one having no significance or value of its own. An Elector is chosen because he will vote for a particular candidate; it is precisely the same in result as if the vote were cast directly for that candidate. The Electors do not deliberate together. The day they are returned the Presidential election is over. Every one knows who has been sent to the White House at Washington. The subsequent proceedings of the Electors themselves scarcely attract the least public attention. They send their ballots to the President of the Senate, and I have often been assured by old politicians in the United States that in no known instance has an elector ever voted against the candidate whom he has undertaken to support. Indeed, he is usually as strongly interested as his constituents in the success of the candidate of his party. To break faith would be to ruin him. He would, in the words of one of the first political men in the country, "be hooted out of society." And the authority of Mr. Justice Story confirms this, when he says of the Elector, that the "exercise of an independent judgment would be treated as a political usurpation, dishonourable to the individual, and a fraud upon his constituents."

The President is, therefore, an officer directly elected by the people, and not by a small and picked body. In the words of the learned commentator just quoted, the whole foundation of the system so elaborately constructed has been subverted; but it was impossible to prevent the adoption of the present arrangement. The people were sure to satisfy themselves that the electors would consent to receive instructions, and to take precautions against their breaking faith; nor would it be easy, or perhaps possible, to invent any device which should give the shadow of power to the people, and the substance to the delegates whom they had the unqualified right to appoint.

The mode of electing the Senate has been sufficiently explained. In choosing members for the popular branch of the Legislature the immediate action of the people at the polls is again felt. By the system of apportionment which now prevails, there is one representative to about every hundred thousand persons,[10] and the State is broken

[10] With regard to certain slight inequalities which this plan is found to produce, Webster remarks, "The apportionment of repre-

up into as many districts as it is entitled to return members to Congress, each district returning one member. Thus, the population of the State of New York entitles it to thirty-two representatives, therefore it is divided into thirty-two districts; and when the fact previously mentioned is borne in mind, that the candidate usually resides in his district, and that he is elected only for two years, it will be obvious that the control of the people over their representatives is very great. They are popular or unpopular in an instant. Their votes are carefully watched by the active and never-tiring politicians of their districts, and they are called to account for every error or fault they may commit. The pressure applied to them is constant and not to be eluded. If a member attempts to represent the interests of the nation, unmindful of his constituency, he soon ceases to represent anybody. His first term of office is his last.

The political management and control of every election is exclusively appropriated by the local managers of the party. In every Congressional district there sits a committee which selects the candidate whom it is intended to bring before the people. This process is called the party nomination, and the candidate who hoped to be returned independently of that

---

sentative power can never be precise and perfect. There must always exist some degree of inequality."—Works, iii. 374. The system now practised is perhaps as nearly equal and fair as any other that could be devised.

nomination, or of the committee, or of the faction, would realize in the end that he had spent a large sum of money merely to assure himself of the invincibility of party organizations. On the other hand, the candidate who secures the regular nomination has all the machinery of his party to aid him.[11] His name is included in the general list of the candidates of his party, and the voter takes it and "votes the whole ticket," as it is called, often without knowing anything of the men for whom he is voting, but resting satisfied with the knowledge that they have received the sanction and recommendation of his leaders. The candidate rarely makes an appeal to the body of his constituency. The committee are his masters, and he must settle every detail, and, to borrow the common phrase, "square his opinions" with them. There is no "nomination day" as in England, the candidate is not compelled to appear before his

[11] To appreciate the true character of the nominating convention, it is only necessary to read the following remarks of the 'Nation,' a paper which was the organ of the party in power at the time the article appeared :—"Moreover, it is not the best portion of the convention which does the real work of selection, but a small minority whose chief qualification for the task is skill in that species of jugglery called 'management.' There is no earthly means of knowing beforehand on whom they will fix as a candidate for any office, as they are governed by considerations of all kinds, most of them very low, of which the public outside can see or learn absolutely nothing. So that the voters never know what species of animals they are expected to swallow until a week or two before the election, and after the announcement of the ticket no qualms or hesitation are allowed. You are expected to open your mouth and shut your eyes."—April 11th, 1867.

constituency after the election, and thus there are no opportunities for those disturbances which sometimes scandalize election proceedings in the United Kingdom. It has already been said that the ballot not only fails to provide any security against corruption, but it does not even insure secrecy of voting, nor is any value attached to it in that respect. Temporary stalls are fitted up near the polling-booths, and there the tickets of the respective parties are publicly distributed to the electors. Every one can see to which booth they go for their tickets, and, although they could easily be obtained before the election, yet the common custom is to take them at the booths which are set up for the purpose of affording this accommodation,—in other words, to throw aside as worthless the boasted contrivance for insuring secrecy.

It is often said by politicians who profess to be anxious to make the English elective system identical with the American, that, as the suffrage is extended, corruption is diminished, because it is not practicable to buy and sell large masses of men. Hence, it is affirmed, there is greater purity of election in the United States than in England. Men there are influenced in the choice of public officers solely by patriotic motives. They scorn to receive compensation for their votes. These are statements which only wilful or accidental blindness to the working of the elective franchise in the United States can explain. No American would assert that purity of election is common in his country. There are few of them who will not frankly deplore the low and degraded view of the suffrage which the least cultivated—that is to say, the numerous—classes habitually take. No doubt the evil is seen in its greatest magnitude in cities and large towns, but in America it is not pretended that it is exclusively confined to them. It spreads to the rural districts, and it is constantly extending wider and wider. Men often strive to get returned to the Legislatures of their States chiefly for the sake of profit,—that profit which goes into their pockets, and which they derive from bartering their votes. From the first day they take their seats, they are beset with inducements to support private bills which involve large interests, and in which their own interests are not forgotten. The work of making bargains with the members—of paying them so much money for voting in a particular way—has become an open and a recognised trade. It is not considered dishonourable to take a bribe, and when a man is proved to have taken one he suffers no loss in the public estimation.[12] The professional lobbyist is one of the best known men in America. In the choice of Senators for the Federal Congress, the State Legislatures are often guilty of shameful corruption. An eminent American politician[13] stated in a letter to which his name was attached, that "corruption, bribery, and fraud," had been freely charged, and he

[12] See chapter viii., on "Party Government."

[13] Mr. Thaddeus Stevens.

feared "too often proved to have controlled the actions" of the Legislature of Pennsylvania, the State which this gentleman represented in the House of Representatives, and concerning which he therefore spoke with authority. "A seat in the Legislature," he continued, "became an object of ambition for the chance of levying contributions from rich corporations, and other large jobs." The very office of Senator had been bought and sold for gold.[14] The only surprise that these disclosures occasioned was provoked by the circumstance that any public man should have had the courage to make them. Men enter these State Legislatures poor and leave them rich.[15] It is unnecessary to say that this vicious

---

[14] The whole of the passage from the letter in question is interesting enough to be quoted:—"It cannot be denied, and therefore need not be concealed, that for the last ten or fifteen years the Legislature of Pennsylvania has had a most unenviable reputation. Corruption, bribery, and fraud have been freely charged, and, I fear, too often proved to have controlled their actions. No matter how honest when chosen, the atmosphere of Harrisburg seems to have pierced many of them with a demoralizing taint. A seat in the Legislature became an object of ambition, not for the per diem, but for the chance of levying contributions from rich corporations and other large jobs. Corruption finally became so respectable as to seduce candidates for office boldly to bid for them, and to pay the cash for the delivery of the ballot. The very office of Senator is known to have been once bought with gold, and to have been trafficked for on other memorable occasions in exchange for the precious metals. Indeed, it has become proverbial that the longest purse is sure to win." This letter was published in the Washington 'Morning Chronicle,' 7th Jan. 1867.

[15] A letter in the 'New York Tribune,' dated Albany, March 18, 1867, exposes many instances of corruption which have been practised in the New York Legislature. Not forty men in that body, the writer states, could have been found for ten years past willing to

debasement of an honestly designed elective system is not to be ascribed to any peculiarity in the American character. There the poor are no worse than they are anywhere else; in some respects they are even better fitted to be intrusted with political power. It is the result of the wide and indiscriminate suffrage which has been adopted in the country. The same consequences would be likely to follow from the operation of the same system in every part of the world.

---

vote without a bribe. The New York Central Railroad Company has paid since 1853 half a million of dollars in corrupting the members. One Senator demanded 25,000 dollars for his vote on a particular bill. In a subsequent letter, published in the 'Tribune' of March 29, 1867, the same writer asserts that this railway company paid away 100,000 dollars to "legislators and outsiders." A bill was passed through the Senate at a cost of 40,000 dollars. In the Assembly "between forty and fifty votes were paid for, at prices varying from 300 to 1500 dollars each." And in a third letter, published in the 'Tribune' of the 3rd April, 1867, the writer says:—"During all the many years that I have been accustomed to observe the character of legislators and the proceedings of the body, I have never seen anything to compare with the present assemblages of representatives in point of shamelessness, rapacity, and recklessness of consequences. Their predecessors have often been noted for venality and greediness, but these people sell their votes openly, haggle about the price without pretence of concealment, and then boast of what they have been paid." The 'New York Times' of April 8, 1867, confirms all these statements. "We venture to say," says the writer, "that, as a general rule, for the last ten years, one-fifth of the members of each House have been in the habit of taking bribes for their votes—the fact is open, notorious to every one who has had any personal connection with Albany legislation." And again:—"We speak what hundreds of men know, from personal experience, that no bill whose passage will confer pecuniary advantage upon any man or any corporation can be passed in Albany except by bribery—except by paying members to pass it. No man can get his rights, or prevent serious damage to his private interests, or avert ruin from himself and his family, except by bribery."

If seats in the State assemblies are worth a large price, it may be inferred that a seat in the Federal Congress is a still more precious commodity; and in truth the traffic for it scarcely ever ceases. When the candidate is returned, he must go on making it "worth the while" of his friends to support him, or his next election is placed in great jeopardy. But bribery is a penal offence in the United States, and through this misfortune the candidate is driven to great exercises of ingenuity in order to pay the price demanded of him without detection. Various stratagems are employed by both candidate and elector. In the first place, the candidate deals with the representatives of small associations, not with individuals. The foreman of a manufactory, or of a fire company, goes to him, and says, "There are twenty or thirty of us who are going to vote for this election, and we do not much care on which side. We rather prefer you, and if you will give us so much we will vote for you." Or, again, the candidate makes a heavy bet against or upon his own success with some man who has the control over fifty votes, and pays the bribe over in that form. I was once shown by a candidate a large number of tickets for a ball (which was a ball purely of the imagination, and never intended to be held), that he had been obliged to buy from some one who had twenty votes at his command. Buying tickets for a ball is not a penal offence in the United States.

Another ingenious scheme for plundering a contestant, is to bring forward what is called a "split candidate." A certain number of electors, having a mind to profit by their electoral privileges, meet together and agree to start an opposition candidate in the field. He is kept "running" until he is likely to divide the constituency, and then he is bought off by the first candidate, who may find it necessary to open his purse for the same purpose more than once during the election. Any party manager who chose to be candid could give various other illustrations of expedients for bribing which are practised with much skill and success in America. Spurious votes are manufactured, and in the large cities personification of dead or absent persons, and the forging of naturalization papers, are among the most commonplace incidents of an election. Each side stations detectives, or other agents, at the polling-booths to watch for counterfeit voters. Sometimes whole masses of men are transported from one district to another, a process which has been named, after the inventor, "gerry-mandering." It is needless to explore further into these dark recesses of political depravity. It is not a matter of satisfaction to find that a great plan for popular government, devised by men of noble character and purpose, is dishonoured by those to whom it has descended, and made to appear beneath its proper merit in the estimation of the world.

The result of government by numbers is written in those public records which few men in America have the time or the inclination to search—namely, the annals of Congress. There may be found revelations of legislative corruption without a parallel in recent times, while the statute-books bear evidence of the careless and irresponsible manner in which the hired representatives of the people fulfil their appointed tasks. The history of the United States government proves nothing so clearly as that the uncontrolled supremacy of the masses leads to the introduction into political life of a class of men who would certainly be rejected by an educated and intelligent constituency. It gives rise to an overbearing intolerance of the opinions of others, to unworthy views of public station, to the suppression of independent thought, and to the political banishment of men whose superior talents and elevated principles might enable them to render the greatest service to the Republic. Probity and high intelligence are qualities which have less influence in deciding the course of an election than the command of wealth, or a flexible adaptibility to the temper of the hour, and a skilful subserviency to the popular wishes. What the bulk of electors look for is a man, not of great capabilities, but of pliant intellect and malleable convictions. And thus no past labours, be they ever so successful, will save a man from disgrace the moment he dares to oppose his opinions to those of the multitude, while the truculent and designing demagogue, who flatters the ignorant by anticipating their desires, is lifted into favour and power.

The very principles of the government are repudiated or vindicated according to the caprice of the moment. Freedom of opinion is punished by public odium and the sacrifice of name and reputation.[16] The man who ventures to stand in the path of the majority is swept away and disappears probably for ever—for in these contests the victors imitate the tactics of their Indian foes on the frontier, who either slaughter their enemies outright, or leave them incapable of doing further harm. They are poisoned with bitter slanders and revilings. The identical ills which Montesquieu saw were incidental to a democracy, seem to be inseparable from political life in America. Every citizen thinks he is wiser than the ruler, and would fain rule him. "Then the people, incapable of bearing the very power they have delegated, want to manage everything themselves—to debate for the Senate, to execute for the magistrate, and to decide for the judges. The people are desirous of exercising the functions of the magistrates, who cease to be revered."[17] These are the stains upon a system sometimes alleged to be purity itself, and Americans of the better class are anxious rather to remove them than to deny their existence.

The perception of the disadvantages which so ex-

---

16 Daniel Webster, because he saw reason to modify his opinions on the slavery question before his death, is constantly vilified, and every feature of his private character assailed. See, for an example, 'North American Review' for January, 1867.

17 'Esprit des Lois,' liv. viii. chap. ii.

tended a suffrage entail upon the people is not confined to foreign observers. In America also they are understood and regretted. That the Federal Legislature was a body characterized by greater dignity and ability thirty years ago than it is now is generally admitted. The standard of public life has fallen. Chancellor Kent saw the change that was going on in his day with evident misgiving and alarm. It could not then be traced to the effect of a great revolution, as some might be disposed to trace it now. "Such a rapid course of destruction of the former constitutional checks," he writes, "is matter for grave reflection; and to counteract the dangerous tendency of such combined forces as universal suffrage, frequent elections, all offices for short periods, all officers elective, and an unchecked press, and to prevent them from racking and destroying our political machines, the people must have a larger share than usual of that wisdom which is first pure, then peaceable, gentle, and easy to be entreated."[18] But without this wisdom, and there is nothing to prove that it has been rained down, like manna to the Israelites, upon any chosen people, a licensed rule of numbers is one under which great and peculiar wrongs are wrought. The well-instructed, the conscientious, the men of sterling character and means and leisure, are without influence in the State. There is a despotism of the poor over the rich. No party would think of going to the

[18] Kent's 'Commentaries,' vol. i. p. 234, *note*.

better class to choose a candidate for the Presidency. The lower classes are not satisfied with being acknowledged the equals of the upper; they take every opportunity of making them feel that as they are numerically superior, they can and will keep fast hold of the ascendency in the State. It is the fashion to assert that the tendency of the age is towards Democracy, and that it would be well for the world that it should everywhere triumph. Such is not the language heard in America from men competent to form an impartial judgment. There we find them asking, "Is America as peaceable, as orderly, as happy in its internal affairs, as a perfect form of government, aided by unlimited resources, ought to make it? Does it knit all classes together, as European reformers, who desire to see all nations model their governments after our pattern, appear to suppose? Are we quite free from class prejudices, from sectional differences, from jealousies of party and faction? Do we actually place all men on a political equality, or have we only reversed the ancient injustices of class?" And there it is also said, by men of long experience, "The English government is the only one in the world likely to last, and the only one which is just and equal in its treatment of all classes of the people." Nothing is more common than to hear men in positions of the highest authority deplore the fact that there seems no possibility of placing any limits upon the suffrage in America.

An equal representation of the people is not attained under the American system. All the power is lodged in the hands of one class, and that class the one least fit to govern.[19] The House of Commons since the year 1832 has been said to be an epitome of the English nation; the House of Representatives is nothing but a deputation from the least cultivated classes of America. There is no great interest, whether of labour or capital, in the world of commerce or the world of thought, which has not hitherto been faithfully reflected and honestly guarded, without detriment to other interests, in the House of Commons. Property does not obtain all the representation, and even the men who are supposed to represent property are not as a rule unwilling to do justice to labour. Learning is not without the influence which justly belongs to it, and although it may have been that there were classes in the nation which were not represented in proportion to their numbers, yet it would be untrue to assert that any class was left totally unrepresented. No one who has seen the American Congress in working, or who is properly aware of the constituents of which it must necessarily be formed, will ever be able to look but with profound anxiety and apprehension upon an attempt to

---

[19] "Those who attempt to level never equalise. In all societies, consisting of various descriptions of citizens, some description must be uppermost. The levellers, therefore, only change and pervert the natural order of things; they load the edifice of society by setting up in the air what the solidity of the structure requires to be on the ground."—Burke's 'Reflections on the Revolution in France.'

make the House of Commons exactly like it. The ignorant choose the ignorant to represent them. Equal suffrage can never lead to equal representation. The class which is no less the honour and mainstay of a nation than the labouring class, are disfranchised, and are rendered utterly powerless to save their country from any dangers which they may see before it. There are able and honest men in Congress, but, like the honest and intelligent electors in a constituency, they have little or no influence, for they are overmatched by numbers. The majority know that to keep their seats it is only necessary to flatter the poorer classes, and pander to their worst prejudices. It is a general and unscrupulous sycophancy of the lowest orders of the community. No other class is worth soliciting, for there is no other which possesses political power. Integrity is regarded as a weakness. Official station is only valued because "it confers the opportunity to make money, and to enrich relatives and friends. The consequence has been a degree of corruption disgraceful to the country and the age. Bribery is almost acknowledged as a part of legislation, whilst dishonest jobs and contracts so abound that they are regarded as things of course." These are not the words of a hater of democracy or of America. It is a description by an American writer of good repute of his own country.[20] And the same writer has the courage

[20] See Fisher's 'Trial of the Constitution' (Philadelphia, 1862) p. 346.

(and it needs no small courage) to tell his countrymen plainly that the English constitution is infinitely wiser, and better for the people, than theirs. "The great uprising of the nation," he says, "is a proof that the electoral machine has not worked well; that if it winnows the opinions of the people, it gives them not the grain but the chaff, and that some other machine is imperatively demanded to represent their intelligence and moral sentiment."[21] The purification of the suffrage is the only conceivable remedy, and that is an impracticable one.

So far, indeed, from restricting the franchise, the irresistible course of events must lead to its indefinite extension. Mr. Justice Story tells us that no one has demanded or conceded the right to universal suffrage; but who is to say to an uncontrolled force, constantly increasing in momentum, Thus far shalt thou come and no farther? The day is not distant when universal suffrage will be demanded by the people, and whenever it is demanded it must be conceded. Already, as we have seen, the door is opened to all comers in some of the Western States. The admission of women and minors to the franchise is constantly discussed as one of the political possibilities of the hour. The Legislature of Kansas has already voted for woman suffrage, and in the New

[21] Ibid. p. 350. See also the New York 'Round Table' of October 5, 1867, in which the following passage occurs:—"The tendency to the elevation of ignorant, superficial, and conceited men to places which can be filled only by the wise and thoughtful is stronger than ever in our country, and our capacity to govern ourselves is growing less every day."

York Convention of 1867, called to revise the State Laws, several propositions were brought forward to admit women, and boys of eighteen, to the privileges of the ballot. The old limitations and restrictions are being contemptuously swept away. "The progress and impulse of popular opinion," laments Chancellor Kent, "is rapidly destroying every constitutional check, every conservative element intended by the sages who framed the earliest American Constitution as safeguards against the abuses of popular suffrage."[22]

It is in vain that the small and almost powerless independent press of the country warns the people of the disastrous effects of the system to which they seem so immoveably attached.[23] The public man

---

[22] 'Commentaries,' i. sect. 582.

[23] The following is an extract from an article entitled 'Delusion as the Basis of Government,' published in the 'Round Table,' New York, Nov. 17, 1866:—

"With every election the evidence accumulates that the framers of our Government reckoned falsely in relying upon the existence among the populace of sufficient discernment of what is for the public good, together with sufficient honesty and patriotism to secure it. Each year shows an increase of ignorance and prejudice among the voters, and a lessened efficiency and integrity among the rulers, until our various legislative bodies, speaking generally, have come to be mere assemblages of incompetent or self-seeking nobodies. It has become of less and less use for educated men to vote; their recommendation of men or measures meets no attention; they seldom have an opportunity to vote for a candidate in whom they can discern fitness for office; and so the higher social classes have pretty much ceased to have anything to do with our government.

"It is all very well for enthusiasts at a distance to hold us forth to audiences also at a distance as an instance of the inseparable connection between popular enlightenment and self-government. The

who ventured to make in his place in Congress a proposition to contract the suffrage would find it impossible to preserve his seat in the assembly. All can see the danger, but none dare attempt to point out the proper means of warding it off. Even the least apprehensive can find no better hope than in the education of the masses. That is their strongest security against the misuse of political power. Before men are fit to exercise the privilege of the suffrage they must be educated, it is said. But meanwhile they are allowed to exercise it. Moreover, unless an educational test be applied, how is the educational qualification of the voter to be ascertained? The masses would resist any such test.

---

incomprehensible national venity which prevents our acknowledging any truths to our disadvantage, has so far concealed from the eyes of the world the growing mistrust by thinking unpolitical Americans of the stability of the imposing fabric we have reared on the sands of popular caprice, that republicanism is considered abroad to have achieved a success of which we at home are by no means so assured. The style of electioneering arguments in vogue in every election, the irrelevant puerilities of the partisan press, the impunity with which it relies upon the credulity and passions of the voters, the ease with which demagogues marshal their rabble to the polls; the fact that the utterly stupid, vicious, and degraded classes of the community can at any time, by sufficiently good management, be made to turn the scale between parties—such considerations as these must convince any mind open to conviction of the futility of hoping to make a safe government of such material.

"Nothing could well be more gloomy than the political prospect which this state of things has procured us. The most persistently sanguine theorists have for some time given over discovering any cheerful promise, or, if they have done so, have found none to attend to them. No party, no statesman, offers us a way of extrication from our perilous situation."

Nothing can be more curious than to mark the visionary and delusive view which some of America's greatest men have taken of the suffrage. The supposition is, Webster tells us, that in using the suffrage "men will act conscientiously, under the influence of public principle and patriotic duty, and that in supporting men or measures there will be a general prevalence of honest intelligent judgment and manly independence." In what age of the world did this eminent statesman suppose that the motives and instincts of mankind would be so supernaturally changed, as to bring them to the practice of these principles? When is this reign of celestial purity and peace to begin, and who is to rule over the kingdom? And is it in an enthusiast's dream only that we can hope to see the American democracy bearing that excellent and perfect fruit which is to satisfy all who partake of it, the rich and the poor, the high and the low, he who has much and he who has little, alike?

It is true that in America the injurious consequences of universal suffrage are modified by the condition of society which has previously been referred to, namely, the distribution of land among small proprietors all over the country. This alone would suffice to prevent that general and periodical wreck of property which some have supposed would be wrought by the free admission of all classes to the franchise. But it does not provide any guarantee that the powers of the government will be intrusted to the most worthy and competent hands. Even in the rural districts, where the strength of the nation really lies, the people may often be led astray by interested politicians, and with the greater facility because of the unsuspiciousness and sincerity of their nature. Removed from the hotbeds of political intrigue, too much occupied in their daily labours to follow the course of minor events, rarely troubling themselves with the extreme views of either party, they are easily amenable to the arguments and representations of a man who comes before them with a specious embodiment of opinions which he has endeavoured to adapt to their prejudices. But, although constituencies may be misled for a time, the common sense of an eminently practical people will prevent a total subversion of the framework of society. The great body of the working classes have a material stake in the well-being and stability of the commonwealth. The most potent of all motives, self-interest, restrains them from running into extreme excesses. Hence the fears which are entertained of universal suffrage in England are unknown in America. In the latter country, there are physical conditions which render the widest extension of the suffrage comparatively harmless. Unless these conditions could be enjoyed in England, and it is impossible that they should be, it is folly to talk of making the English elective system the counterpart of the American. It would be as reasonable to propose to repeat the feudal system in America. The greatest objection of moderate reformers in England to unrestricted suffrage is that the lawful rights of property would be violated. "I entertain no hope," said Lord Macaulay, "that, if we place the government of the kingdom in the hands of the majority of the males of one-and-twenty told by the head, the institution of property will be respected."[24] Such a statement applied to America would be absurd, for there the property is at present distributed among small holders. Not without reason is it contended that a vast revolution would be the ultimate issue of the attempt to engraft Republican theories upon an ancient government. All circumstances must be changed to assure the success of such an experiment. If it were possible to give to England the surplus lands of America, it would be a matter scarcely worth contending for, so far as regards the security of property alone, what form of suffrage should be adopted. In densely populated countries, where periods of distress are liable to recur, the people are apt to turn upon the government and rend it for consequences which no government can avert. Lord Macaulay justly described the conditions which are indispensable to the safe working of unlimited suffrage, when he said, in his speech on Parliamentary Reform in 1831, "If the labourers of England were in that state in which I, from my soul,

[24] Speech on the People's Charter. Works (ed. 1866), vol. viii. p. 222.

wish to see them, if employment were always plentiful, wages always high, food always cheap, if a large family were considered not as an encumbrance but a blessing, the principal objections to Universal Suffrage would, I think, be removed." These have been the advantages possessed by the United States, but it is beyond the power of reformers to bestow them upon England.[25]

The principle of democracy, according to an authority who is never contradicted in America, is that "everybody should be represented, and that everybody should be represented equally."[26] Judged by

---

[25] Those who suppose that in order to remove all causes of discontent in England we have only to adopt the American form of government, would do well to read the debates in the Federal Convention which planned the Constitution. They would there meet with sentiments like the following:—"In his private opinion, he had no scruple in declaring, supported as he was by the opinion of so many of the wise and good, that the British Government was the best in the world, and that he doubted much whether anything short of it would do in America." This was said by Mr. Hamilton. (Madison's 'Reports' (Elliot, v.), p. 202.) Mr. Hamilton represented New York. In the same spirit Mr. Sherman said he thought "the people immediately should have as little to do as may be about the government." Mr. Geary said, "The evils we experience flow from the excess of democracy." Upon the resolution that the House of Representatives should be elected directly by the people instead of by the State Legislatures, as had been proposed, six States voted for, and two (New York and North Carolina) against, while two others (Connecticut and Delaware) were divided. But the principles laid down in the first chapter of this volume were unquestionably those which were held by the majority, and which have ever since governed the country, and derived fresh vitality and force from the lapse of time.

[26] Mr. John Stuart Mill, in the House of Commons, May 30th, 1867.

this standard, the American theory of representation is the greatest fallacy by which an intelligent people has ever been deluded. In other systems minorities are at least partially represented, but in the United States they are practically disfranchised. The best educated, highest minded class in America are unrepresented, not only in Congress, but in the Legislatures of their States. The returns of the election for 1866 will best illustrate the injustice which is done to minorities. Thirteen States (excluding those which seceded, and were entirely unrepresented) were left without a single Democratic member in Congress, although the Democratic vote in each State was very large. To give a few instances—the vote in Iowa was 91,227 Republican and 55,815 Democrat. Had the system worked equitably, the State would have had four Republican members and two Democrats. But the small majority took away the Democratic share, and Iowa was represented by six Republicans. Massachusetts had her entire delegation of ten members Republican, the vote cast being 91,880 to 26,671—and thus the minority ought to have had two members and the majority eight only. In New York the proportionate representation in Congress would have been sixteen Republicans and fifteen Democrats, the vote being 366,315 on the Republican against 352,526 on the Democratic side. The actual representation of the minority was only *eleven*, the majority gaining twenty members. In Pennsylvania the vote was 307,274 against 290,096, and the representation was eighteen to six, whereas it should have been thirteen to eleven. In this last case the majority was only 8587 votes—or about one vote in a thousand of the voting population of the State—and by that it gained five members more than it was fairly entitled to. The State of Ohio was represented by three Democrats and sixteen Republicans—and yet the Democratic voters numbered 211,690, and the Republicans no more than 254,090. Take another instance: in the thirty-ninth Congress[27] 1,600,000 voters in the North and West gained only thirty representatives in Congress, while 2,000,000 voters in the same section of country were represented by 128 members.

These inequalities, and many others which might be cited, have more than once been the subject of discussion in Congress, and various means of redressing the injustice to the minority have been proposed. One of the most recent of these attempts was made in the United States Senate by a member[28] who proposed the adoption of the system of cumulative voting, beginning with the Southern States, which, being absolutely under the control of Congress, are deemed a convenient subject for any experiments. It was urged that the majority in a Congressional district, however small, obtained the whole representation of that district, whereas, if people were allowed to vote upon the cumulative plan, the mino-

[27] 1865-67. [28] Senator Buckalew, on the 11th July, 1867.

rity would be able to secure at least one member. But the Senate declined to take any step towards the proposed reform, and the governing party of the day is never likely to assent to a change which would be its own death-blow at the next election.[29]

[29] The following extracts, from a report of the Personal Representation Society of New York, to the Constitutional Convention of 1867, fully substantiate the charges made against the representative system of the United States:—

"It is a bold thing to say that throughout the Union our civil policy in regard to representation is a mistake and therefore a failure, but a slight examination of the principles upon which representation is based may serve to convince you, as it has served to convince us, of this truth. If we were to draw a bill of indictment against our present electoral scheme, we should first and foremost set forth that it is a sham, that it is not what it pretends to be, that it does not effect the representation of the people, but only a part of the people. We have shown that our present system is unphilosophical, and results in evils so flagrant and so manifest, that they not only make our legislation and the venality of our legislators a by-word and a reproach, but also retard the progress of republican and democratic institutions the world over, by having the evils, arising from our faulty system of election, laid to the door of democracy itself."

CHAPTER VIII.

PARTY GOVERNMENT.

ALREADY we have repeatedly found it necessary to dwell upon the evil results which flow from the organization and supremacy of party rule in the United States. That rule has done more than anything else to pervert the true principles of the government. It has lowered and changed the original character of those national institutions to which men like Washington, and Hamilton, and Madison were most deeply attached. It takes possession of the entire political system, and wrests it into an instrument for the advancement of personal interests. A rapid and incessant deterioration is progressing in each department of the public service. There are still some countries left in the world in which the history of great parties is a portion of the history of great principles and ideas, for which a persistent, if not always a generous, struggle is kept up generation after generation.[1] In America it is a record

[1] See, for example, Mr. Wingrove Cooke's 'History of Party' in England (Lond. 1832). But, probably, could this author have lived to bring his work down to the present time, the moral of it would be very different.

of perpetual contests for the aggrandisement of individuals, who at the best unworthily reflect sectional discords and hatreds, and of cliques which know no sentiment higher than that of securing power in order that profit may be gained by it. Hence, the least deserving men too often contrive to seize the leadership. They govern their forces with a rod of iron, and do not hesitate to adopt the most unscrupulous expedients to extend their sphere of dominion. According to Burke, "party is a body of men united for promoting, by their joint endeavours, the national interest, upon some particular principle in which they are all agreed." . It is not too much to affirm that politicians seldom rise to this view of party in the American republic. Many turn to public life distinctly and avowedly as a means of making money. It is a paying trade. Self-interests are the first consideration; the interest of the nation is entirely secondary, and sometimes it is impossible to detect the evidence of its being taken into account at all. An English historian may see abundant cause, in looking back upon the great victories or defeats which have chequered the course of party in his country, to exclaim, "By argument and discussion truth is discovered, public opinion is expressed, and a free people are trained to self-government. Who can fail to recognise in party the very life-blood of freedom?"[2] No such eulogy will ever be

[2] T. Erskine May's 'Constitutional History of England,' chapter viii., *conclusion*.

pronounced upon party in America by the candid and truthful historian. There, argument and discussion are easily suppressed in the popular branch of the Legislature, and a tyranny unheard of under other constitutional governments is imposed upon the minority. The circumstances amid which Congress does its daily work reflect greater light on these abuses of power than general statements could do, and a short account of them will tell its own story.[3]

The House of Representatives is sufficiently spacious to seat the 658 members of the House of Commons instead of its own 277 members. It is lit from the roof, the windows being of ground and stained glass, with copies of the arms of each State in the centre of the squares. The Speaker sits close to the wall under one of the galleries, with a large brass eagle and two flags above his head. The desks of the members are placed in a semicircle in front of the Speaker, and around the hall run the galleries for strangers, large enough to hold 1500 persons. People walk in and out as they please; the only restriction being that into some galleries men cannot go unless they are accompanied by ladies. There is sometimes much noise and confusion in these public galleries, and very often the discussions below are interrupted by applause. In the Senate (which is in outward peculiarities only a smaller copy of the

[3] The descriptions here given were written by the author in the course of several Sessions, and are now partly borrowed from his letters to 'The Times.'

House) these demonstrations are always promptly suppressed, and indeed in that Chamber the proceedings are invariably conducted with greater order and dignity than in the other. But it must be borne in mind that there are only sixty Senators at present entitled to seats, and of this number there are often scarcely a score in their places except when votes are being taken, whereas there are in the House a hundred and ninety-one Representatives, most of them present every day. The eighty-six members representing the Southern States are excluded.

Upon the opening of a new Session the Speaker of the House is elected by ballot. The oldest "consecutive" member swears him in, and afterwards the Speaker administers the oath to all the members. He does not wear any distinctive dress, and, when he is tired of occupying the Chair, he sends a message to any member he may please to select, and places him in authority over the House for that day only. He generally alludes to himself as the "Chair," in this form—"The Chair thinks the ayes have it," or "The Chair does not hear any gentleman object;" and his decision on a point of order, or upon any other question that may arise, is not final, but may be disputed by any member. It is then put to the House whether it will support the Speaker's decision or not, and if, on a division, the votes are equal, the Speaker can give the casting vote sustaining his decision—an incident which has happened on several occasions. The Speaker is also at liberty to vacate the Chair, and join at any time in the debates. He has great control over the management of a discussion, by being able to call upon speakers of his own party rather than upon the opposition, but this advantage is not always allowed to be exercised. An able speaker, sure of commanding the attention of the House, cannot be suppressed by these rough devices. In restoring order the Speaker knocks on his desk with a hammer, and occasionally has to knock loud and often before his appeals are heeded. This is also the custom in the Senate, and the method of conducting business is almost identical in both Chambers.

When a division is demanded, there are three ways of taking the votes. First, the members stand up and are counted by the Speaker; but if any member is not satisfied, he may demand tellers, whereupon two members are named by the Speaker, and the House passes between them. Or a member may demand the "yeas and nays," and if one-fifth of the House sustains the demand (which the Speaker can tell by his eye, the assenting members holding up their hands) the names are called over, and by the rules each member is compelled to vote, unless he is excused by the House—but this is not adhered to. A member may let his name be called and make no answer, and yet have his vote recorded when the roll is finished, by rising in his place—having, perhaps, been anxious to see first how his colleagues, or the members of his own way of thinking, intended to vote. In the House, members appear to be allowed to speak as often as they please to the same Bill, but the Senate has a rule that "no member shall speak more than twice in any one debate on the same day, without leave of the Senate." Unless upon the specific demand of a member, the rules are seldom rigorously enforced. In the House, a member is not allowed to speak longer than an hour at one time, unless special permission be given. A member may only desire to speak for five minutes, but, having obtained possession of the floor, he has a right to hold it for a full hour, and he may divide the surplus of his time among his friends. Thus it is very common to hear a member say, "I yield the floor for ten minutes to the member from Maine," "Now I yield it for five minutes to the member from Pennsylvania," and so on, till he has accommodated all his friends, or his hour is expired. The Speaker, of course, decides when each member's allotted portion of the hour is gone.

The patience with which even the dreariest of speakers is tolerated, both in the Senate and the House, is one of the most striking features of Congress. A member pulls out an immense roll of manuscript, and endeavours to arouse himself into animation over the sentences which he has laboriously prepared. The House cannot be said to listen to what he says, but it is perfectly quiet, and never interrupts. These essays are all printed *in extenso* in the 'Congressional Globe,' and thus an insignificant member is often reported through fifteen or twenty columns of this paper, at the expense of the Government, it need scarcely be said. Sometimes a member asks permission of the House to take his speech as read, and it is then printed in the 'Globe' as if it had been actually delivered. It will be obvious at once how much this arrangement encourages laxity of debate, and how hopeless would be the attempt to confine members to the subject before the House. The Government pays the proprietors of the 'Globe' a stated price for every printed column, and it takes in addition five-and-twenty copies of each day's issue for every member.

All through the Session of Congress, there are certain days set apart in the House of Representatives for the convenience of members who wish to make known their views on public affairs. They are called "speech days," and at the beginning of the Session every member who intends to address the House has his name entered upon a list which is afterwards kept by the Speaker. This list is constantly lengthening, for one day will only get rid of perhaps half-a-dozen names, while in the course of a week twenty new ones will be added, so that at the close of a Session there is hardly any hope for the members who stand last on the roll. The names are called by the Speaker in the order in which they are entered, and it often happens that a gentleman is required to deliver an essay which he prepared four months before, and which has little or no bearing upon any question of the hour. On these occasions the House has a deserted and sombre appearance; oftentimes there are not more than forty members present, who are lost in that large chamber, and they amuse themselves by reading the newspapers or writing letters. The Speaker writes his letters also, merely pausing to look at what time a speaker begins, and to knock with his hammer when the prescribed hour is expired. The members understand thoroughly that they are not to look for the attention of the House, but to have their speeches printed in the 'Globe,' so that they can send them to their constituents, and with that arrangement they are perfectly satisfied. The tone of these effusions may be judged of from a few quotations.

"The traitor's voice is hushed, and must be silent for ever; the green grass which grows upon the patriot's grave, the flowers which bloom around their resting-places, shall wave in the triumph of freedom, and the whirlwind and the thunder-cloud as they sweep past their tombs re-echo with tones that will shake the world."[4]

"What name but anarchy, rampant and flagrant anarchy, over which the fallen spirits and incarnate devils might hold a jubilee, would you give to such a state of affairs as this? A little hell in the family all the time! Oh, what a glorious Government that would be! Freedom's soil beneath our feet! and freedom's banner streaming o'er us! The home of the free and the hope of the brave!"[5]

---

[4] Speech of Mr. McKee, of Kentucky.

[5] Mr. Dumont, of Indiana.

"The Constitution of our country was formed upon the model which the great Architect of the universe established when He formed this planetary system of ours."[6]

If these "occasional" days seem often to justify the traditional impressions of Congress — namely, that it is a scene of confusion, in which wild declamation and nonsense are all that can be heard,— it ought to be remembered that the other five days of the week are far more calculated to show that these impressions are erroneous. They are formed upon exceptional incidents, such as some of those which have been described. As a general rule, there is no want of dignity or ability in the manner in which public business is conducted in the Capitol. The man of common sense is always sure of finding an appreciative audience, and there are many men in both Chambers, whose powers as public speakers, and whose great natural talents, would elevate them to a distinguished position wherever they might be placed. Congress has its ludicrous side, like all other large assemblies, and those who wish to form a fair estimate of it should keep away from it on the days when inferior members, or exceptional circumstances, present it in a partial and unfair light. But there is no redeeming circumstance in the measures which are taken by the dominant party to suppress discussion. They give

---

[6] Mr. Hogan.

rise at times to scenes which ought never to be witnessed in a legislative body. An illustration is of greater value than an argument, and I shall therefore give an account of a spectacle which I witnessed in the month of January, 1867.

The occasion of this struggle was the introduction of a Bill from the Judiciary Committee, intended to do away with the effect of a decision in the Supreme Court as to the illegality of the Test Oath. The Bill provided that no person should be permitted to act as attorney or counsellor in any court of the United States who had been guilty of treason or engaged in rebellion, or given aid and comfort to the participants in rebellion. In short, it was intended to prevent, by Act of Congress, any Southern man or Southern sympathizer who happened to be a lawyer from practising his profession,—thus, as a Republican member afterwards said, depriving thousands of families of their bread.

This measure a distinguished Republican, in behalf of the Committee, determined to force through the House the afternoon it was brought forward, without allowing a word of discussion upon it. Some of his own party, with a better sense of reason and justice, strongly condemned this course. He was implored by the Democratic members to yield one hour only for debate, but, confident in the power of his party, he declined. To two or three members he dealt out "five minutes," "three minutes," and to one gentleman "two minutes," and with this concession he deemed the rights of a deliberative assembly were complied with. That immense proportion of the people then represented in Congress who were opposed to this Bill were granted, through their representatives, about ten minutes to consider its provisions.

The minority, for the sake of their own honour, could not suffer this Bill to be read three times in a quarter of an hour without making an attempt to arrest it. They knew they were not strong enough in the House to prevent its passing in the end, and they promised that if they were allowed one hour for debate they would interpose no further opposition. The offer was contemptuously rejected by the other side. "We will keep you here till you pass it," said the Republicans. "Then, you shall keep us here a week," said the Democrats. The only way in which the minority could postpone a division on the Bill, was by bringing forward a series of motions to adjourn, and other resolutions intended only to cause delay. These manœuvres were at once put into practice. On every motion the minority demanded what is called the "yeas and nays"—that is, that the roll of the House shall be read, and each member answer to his name. This most tedious process occupies nearly half-an-hour, and it was repeated no less than 25 times before either side became tired out. The great burden of the struggle fell more upon the Democrats than upon the Republicans, for several reasons. The majority had force enough to admit of relays going out of the House and obtaining refreshments. The minority needed every one of their little band constantly in his place to sustain the demand for the yeas and nays, for which purpose a *fifth* of the entire number present must vote. The minority had a very few more than that fifth, and therefore they could not leave their posts. Then, again, the brunt of the fight fell upon them on account of a form of the House which the majority exercised against them. When the yeas and nays are asked for, a fifth must vote to sustain the demand, and if there is a dispute tellers are required, and the House is counted in that way. Every time the minority called for the yeas and nays the majority made them march between the tellers, and this undesirable exercise was kept up all day and all night, on the meagre nourishment of a few biscuits and a glass of water; while the majority sat comfortably in their arm-chairs, with a good dinner to keep them in an even temper. The Democrats, however, kept to their hard work with unconquerable resolution. Amid many gibes from the Republicans, they went through their dreary rounds between the tellers, and made use of every Parliamentary expedient to delay action upon the Bill. More than once they repeated their offer to give way if but one short hour was allowed them for discussion. In a tone of ridicule and exultation the Radicals refused.

About eight o'clock in the evening, when the House had been in session eight hours, a large proportion of the Radicals had made their escape from the House, and seeing this the Democrats demanded a call. This, of course, necessitated another division, but the roll was called, and the Sergeant-at-Arms despatched for the absent members. To bring them together was an operation which required an hour or two to complete. At 12 o'clock, and again at 3, this process was repeated, members being brought from their beds back to the House.

The Speaker was present the greater part of the night, and did his utmost to preserve order. Sometimes the House presented the appearance of a common bar-room, and once the Speaker was obliged to interfere to put an end to smoking by the members. Not far from the doors it was understood that a couple of whisky bottles were kept well filled by some attendant, who had suddenly started this business on his own responsibility. The town was ransacked for supplies of provisions for the restaurant below, and the members incessantly tried their powers in the manufacture of jokes. One gentleman moved that the President's Message be read. A delinquent member being brought in by the Serjeant-at-Arms, it was moved that he be released on payment of the usual fees, whereupon a motion was made to amend by adding the following:—"And, being subjugated, he shall submit to suffrage without regard to race or colour, and shall take the test oath." Once a number of members began to sing, in an under tone, "Home, sweet home," and a Republican proposed that the Democrats should sing the following verse:—

"And are we wretches yet alive,
And do we still rebel?
'Tis only by amazing grace
That we are out of hell."

Another gentleman offered to read the manuscript of a sermon by the chaplain, but this proposition was hastily declined. On the following day much time was spent in punishing members who had absented themselves without leave, and more than once during the same session the contest was repeated on a lesser scale.

De Tocqueville, who thought that a spirit of national morality was fostered by general equality of rank and station, was compelled to own that this source of virtue failed in political life. "I know of no country," he says in one place, "in which there is so little independence of mind and real freedom of discussion as in America." And again he says, "Freedom of opinion does not exist in America." "I attribute the small number of distinguished men in political life to the ever-increasing despotism of the majority in the United States."[7] In this, the most open and candid of all the chapters in M. De Tocqueville's work, he describes the result of his observations in America without attempting to bring them into unison with his preconceived opinions. This portion of his treatise is rather a narrative than a philosophical essay. He tells us what he saw, and

[7] Vol. i., chap. xv., pp. 337 and 340. (Tome ii., pp. 149 and 153.)

how it affected his mind. One of his American critics has remarked, with great force, that "his practical observations are independent of his abstract theories, and his abstract theories have no connexion with his practical observations." Hence, in his remarks on the omnipotence of the majority, he contradicts many statements concerning the United States which he advanced in other portions of his work. He had seen with his own eyes the intolerance of party spirit in America, the suppression of free discussion, the erection of the worst form of despotism in the midst of a democracy, and under the title of liberty; and he was compelled to acknowledge that the discovery shocked and alarmed him. Had he spoken yet more plainly, his observations would have gained in usefulness, although his popularity might have been diminished. The American writer just quoted frankly says, "If his studies had been more protracted, more patient, more profound, and more consistent in their results, his book would have given far less satisfaction to the people of the United States. For they would not have borne from him, nor from any other man, without deep offence, the truth, the whole truth, and nothing but the truth. Nor would his work have been hailed with such universal applause by the friends of democracy throughout the civilized world."[8] The ordinary American does not give himself time to hear both

[8] 'Southern Review,' April, 1867. (Baltimore, 1867.)

sides of a question. He is quite satisfied with hearing the side which adapts itself to his prejudices and inclinations. The writings of his public journals are too often mere partisan appeals to his passions. The majority alone can make itself fully heard, for no one listens to the minority even when it is allowed a free voice. Burke maintained that this overbearing spirit was inseparable from a democracy,[9] and assuredly there is nothing quite equal to it anywhere in the world outside the United States. Mindful of the warning contained in the words of the American writer just referred to, I borrow also from an American an account of his country in respect of this particular abuse of liberty:—"It might easily be shown that every page of the history of the United States is written all over with the phrase,—the tyranny of the majority. The resolutions and acts of State Legislatures, the proceedings of local and of general Conventions, and, above all, the unread and silent annals of Congress, are each and all everywhere replete with the most melancholy proofs of the tyranny of the majority."[10]

---

[9] "Of this I am certain, that in a democracy the majority of the citizens is capable of exercising the most cruel oppressions upon the minority, whenever strong divisions prevail in that kind of polity, as they often must; and that oppression of the minority will extend to far greater numbers, and will be carried on with much greater fury, than can almost ever be apprehended from the dominion of a single sceptre. In such a popular persecution, individual sufferers are in a much more deplorable condition than in any other."—Burke, 'Reflections on the Revolution in France.'

[10] 'Southern Review,' Vol. i. p. 314.

Any writer might well despair of conveying to those who have not examined closely and minutely into the subject for themselves, an adequate conception of the intolerance and the corruption which prevail in the political life of America. There is no point of view from which the observer sees the character of the people at so great a disadvantage as this. A relentless and implacable spirit animates political opponents. One faction pursues the other with fierce and uncompromising hatred, and adopts a thousand mean and dishonest expedients to destroy it. These offences may not be absent from party tactics elsewhere, but they are seen under peculiarly odious circumstances in America. The ordinary courtesies of life are too frequently violated in the Legislature. For a man to call his opponent a "traitor," and for the other to denounce his accuser as a "liar," causes scarcely any discomposure in the Chamber.[11] There is an utter absence of any high or generous feeling as the standard of public life. "Destroy your adversary, blacken his character, injure his name, do anything to him but allow him fair speech and fair play,"—such is the advice that a leader of party might appropriately give if he were training a set of young politicians for the arena at the Capitol. No matter which side obtains the upper hand, a remorseless tyranny is immediately set

[11] See the 'Congressional Globe' for 1866-67, where several cases of this kind are reported. In one instance a member caned another on the steps of the Capitol (July, 1866).

in action. The antagonists sometimes end by destroying each other. The remnant of a shattered force reappears after an interval in altered dress and under a new name. The leaders watch the current of popular opinion, and try to swim with it, and according to their dexterity, their quickness of sight, and their flexibility of moral temperament, do they lose or recover the direction of affairs. Meanwhile, the people think they govern, and know that they actually can govern whenever they choose to stretch forth their hands. High-principled and honourable men there of course are in American parties, but by what colleagues, what associates, are they surrounded! How repulsive are the avenues by which alone they can pass to distinction! However incorruptible and sturdy, however unassailable in his own principles, an American politician may be, he must often feel discouraged and humiliated when he looks round upon the men with whom he is obliged to act, and makes himself acquainted with the conditions upon which their support and fidelity must be purchased.

This vitiation of the true theory of the Republic by the struggles of parties was not unforeseen in the first days of its trial. Madison was obliged to make the confession that "complaints are everywhere heard from our most considerate and virtuous citizens . . . . that the public good is disregarded in the conflicts of rival parties; and that measures are too often decided, not according to the rules of justice, and the rights of the minor party, but by the supreme force of an interested and overbearing majority."[12] This eminent man believed that the remedy would be found in the extended area of the country, and the wide range over which party conflicts would have to be fought. By what process of reasoning he arrived at this conclusion it is hard to conjecture. The diffusion of parties is a cause of strength instead of weakness. The wider they are distributed, the more powerful they become, and nothing can be easier than to concentrate their energies upon particular localities when the occasion requires. It is no disadvantage to a general to have abundant reserves always at his command. The stringency of party discipline in America prevents a wide dispersion of partisans from being a source of embarrassment. In every State, in every county, in every town, there is a rallying-point for the adherents of each side. The press is active and well supported, the emoluments at the disposal of the party in power flow safely into distant channels, and the man who does his work knows that he is sure of his pay. He is not so far removed from the centre of government that it is safe for his leaders to treat him with neglect or ingratitude. Party was not destined to go through a purification by the means which Madison suggested. Only by the introduction into political life of men of a higher class

---

[12] 'Federalist,' No. 10.

than the average of those who now take part in it was that result attainable. But, as it has been shown, the popular prejudice against the higher class is becoming deeper and stronger. Men who are capable of elevating the political life of the country are deterred from approaching it by the spiteful and malicious horde of demagogues who surround it and claim it as their own. Once in the Senate, a man may serve his country with fearlessness and honour. But the road to the Senate, as we have seen, is too often paved with gold, and the gold has to come from the pocket of the candidate.

But, whatever detriment faction might work in other departments of the Government, it could never affect the choice of the Executive. That office must always remain unsullied and beyond reproach. So the framers of the Constitution dreamed, with a delusive hope in their own work. The "process of election affords a moral certainty, that the office of President will seldom fall to the lot of any man who is not in an eminent degree endowed with the requisite qualifications. Talents for low intrigue, and the little arts of popularity, may alone suffice to elevate a man to the first honours of a single State; but it will require other talents, and a different kind of merit, to establish him in the esteem and confidence of the whole Union."[13] In this supposition Hamilton was as deplorably deceived as Madison had

[13] 'Federalist,' No. 68.

been in his imagined remedy for party delinquencies. The Executive is not chosen by the "whole Union." He is picked up by a party from no one knows where, and tossed into his position no one knows why. Months before the day of nominal election, each faction looks out carefully for a candidate. The first requisite is that he shall be comparatively obscure; the second that he shall be of a plastic disposition. When found, he is kept in dark places until the time is ripe for his adoption and public appearance. He is not allowed to open his lips until the signal is given by his managers. A large staff of agents is scattered over the country to advocate his claims, and disparage those of the opposition candidate.[14] The people cannot bring forward a candidate of their own. Neither can a man offer himself as President without receiving a party nomination, and the strongest party of the hour, not that which produces the ablest man, gains the day. It is a matter of chance what kind of man is placed in the position of chief magistrate. An American writer truly remarks, "Mr. Lincoln was an accident, and the apparatus which turned up his name had before given us Polk, Pierce, and Buchanan. Mr. Lincoln was not really chosen by the people, not

---

[14] Mr. Fisher says,—"An immense force, numbering hundreds of thousands, composed of office-holders and office-seekers, organized, disciplined, and trained for the work, is enlisted for the express purpose of carrying the election of a President."—(Fisher's 'Trial of the Constitution,' p. 262.)

even by those who voted for him." [15] The party convention is the actual elective machine.

The President thus chosen never regains his independence. He remains the mere puppet of the men who placed him in authority, or, if he venture to exercise a will and an opinion of his own, his lot is soon made an unenviable one. "It is certainly desirable," said Hamilton, "that the Executive should be in a situation to dare to act on his own opinion with vigour and decision." That theory has not come down to more recent times. Mr. Lincoln was a man of principle, but he was also the most docile instrument of party that ever lay ready to the hand of aspiring politicians. In no single instance, till near the end of his days, did he ever run counter to the opinions and wishes of the Republican leaders. Repeatedly he gave way to the solicitations or peremptory demands of his friends against his own judgment. He refused for months to issue an Emancipation Proclamation, and at last, when he consented, he spoke privately of it with a sneer. It would be of no more avail, he said, than the Pope's Bull against the comet.[16] When he announced the establishment of the blockade, a leading Radical called upon him and told him the act was a great mistake. "Ah, that," said the President with a laugh, "is Seward's work. I have nothing to do with it." "But," returned his visitor, "you are a lawyer your-

---

[15] Fisher's 'Trial of the Constitution,' p. 265.

[16] See 'Life of Lincoln,' by Hon. H. J. Raymond.

self—you know this cannot stand." "No, I am no lawyer," replied Mr. Lincoln; "I have conducted a few cases about cattle straying or injured fences, but I don't know much about it." And he told one of his quaint stories, and there the matter ended.[17] He did what he was told. A man who would be called a "good President" must be content to follow his example, provided he is on the side of the strong. If he is on the side of the weak he had better go over to the strong. Mr. Lincoln began to exercise an opinion of his own just after the war, with regard to the reconstruction of the insurrectionary States. A portion of his own party immediately turned round upon him and attacked him with the ferocity characteristic of disappointed politicians, and had he lived longer, and persevered in his policy, he might have found himself covered with the odium which fell upon his successor. The President, under the present system, is the nominee of a party, and the creature of that party during the days of his power. If he attempts to break away from it he ruins himself, and the agencies which created him are immediately set in action to overthrow him.

No less is it party which regulates the legislative department of the government.[18] The members

---

[17] This incident was related to me by a Republican Senator, who had been a close friend of Mr. Lincoln's.

[18] This is a topic which has been discussed in previous pages, and it is here reverted to for the sake of completing the general view of party government, and of adducing additional proofs of the statements in the text.

chosen are commonly the mouthpieces of a faction, or the compliant tools of corrupt placemen. It would be strange if there were no upright men in Congress, but no one knows better than such men how weak they are, how little regarded, how hopelessly in the minority.[19] They must become the vassals of their leaders, or sacrifice their seats. While they can conscientiously obey this dictation there is no impropriety committed, but some measure is sure to be brought forward of which they disapprove, and then their convictions are abandoned. There is no help for them. They want, for various reasons, to be in

---

[19] Mr. Fisher says,—"In America the Senate represents the States as such, the House the people, the President the people; but really and practically they all represent a party, because elected by a party. . . . Neither of them is elevated above the reach of party influence—that is to say, of capricious, passionate, often ignorant and reckless, popular influence. Neither of them expresses the idea of nationality, of endurance. Neither of them can be a secure shelter for a minority, for a defeated and oppressed party, or a menaced or oppressed class."—'Trial of the Constitution,' p. 72. See also the following:—"Judging the system of representation now in operation by its fruits, and what have we?—a system that has succeeded in placing men into power whose intellectual and moral status is so low, that their success would be impossible in anything but the now muddy stream of politics. Under our present system of majority representation, the necessity of unification and consolidation of party, for the purpose of becoming the dominant power, is so urgent, as non-success means non-representation, that party discipline becomes almost as rigorous as that of an army; and all men of independence of thought, who, agreeing with a strong minority of a majority upon some of the party measures, while disagreeing as to others, are either compelled to accept the party yoke, however uncomfortably it may fit, and sink their individual opinions, or abstain from taking part in politics."—(From a 'Report of the Personal Representation Society of New York to the Constitutional Convention of 1867.')

Congress, and they can only be there by practising obedience to their chiefs. The forms of Congress, it has been already explained, give the utmost licence to extreme partisans, and allow no freedom to men of moderate opinions. In the election of Speaker by a general vote, the most numerous faction take care that one of their own number shall be appointed. This officer then appoints the Committees which have the first control of every department of business—finance, the tariff, taxation, foreign affairs—and he places upon them a clear majority of his own side. The Committees sit throughout the Session, and no subject which comes within their province can be brought before the House without their consent. Thus, in 1865-7 no member of the minority could bring forward a proposal for the restoration of the Southern States, because by the standing orders it would at once have been referred to the Reconstruction Committee, and there buried out of sight. To render the party discipline more certain in its operation, a "caucus" is held at the beginning of each Session. At this a process akin to swearing in the members is gone through. Each person makes an unexpressed, but well-understood, vow to be true and faithful to his party. The caucus was originally little more important than the preliminary meeting of Conservatives or Liberals which is held at the opening of the English Session at the houses of their respective leaders. It is now a distinct and important part of the governing power of the country. The whole business of the land, at the opening of a Session, is practically at the disposal of a caucus. The deliberations of the body are conducted with closed doors, and the conclusions which have been arrived at are alone made known to the public papers, and often even that dole of information is withheld. The caucus cannot indeed make laws; but when it has decided upon a particular course, it has the power to carry it out, and the people do not learn the motives which led to its adoption. For the sake of avoiding strife and divisions in the party, all the members of it usually attend the caucus, and the weaker section avoids, if possible, a collision with the stronger. This is another evil of the practice of secret discussion, for if it were carried on in the face of day, the minority might often obtain such encouragement and support from without as would enable it to make a successful struggle for its principles. But the dread of the reproach of causing schism and disorganization, and the well-known penalties of offending the leaders, constantly induce even able men to agree to resolutions of which they do not approve, in the hope that when they come before the House an opportunity will arise, or some accident occur, to defeat them.[20] But as a rule no such chance presents itself. The member finds that he has pledged himself to the views of his leaders *en masse*, and no discretionary right of action is afterwards permitted.

---

[20] See 'The Times' (American correspondence) of December 29th, 1865, and March 25th, 1867.

He has accepted sealed orders. A dominant party is not to be assailed lightly or heedlessly. It has ample means with which to harass and destroy the recusant. No wonder, then, that this unseen and potent tyranny infuses a spirit of time-serving and cowardice even into men who enter upon their career firm in their good intentions, and impregnable, as they suppose, in their conscientious principles. They think at first that earnestness of conviction, and resolute adherence to that conviction, will save them from defeat. They soon discover that the virtues by which they set so great a store are ridiculous in the eyes of their party, that they are denounced as visionaries or impostors, that they are impotent against the compact phalanx arrayed before them, and that, so far as their own interests are concerned, they had done better to have entered the Legislature without an opinion to call their own. They go back to their former occupations with a character impaired by the ceaseless assaults and calumnies of their former associates, with old friendships sundered, old ties broken, with discouragement in every circumstance which surrounds them. The member of Congress who aims at being successful, before other considerations, must resolve at the outset to close his eyes and ears to all save those who marshal and lead the columns of his party.[21]

[21] The following is from a Republican paper, the 'New York Evening Post,' of 16th February, 1867:—"The violent and extreme Republicans in both Houses exercise an influence disproportioned to their numbers, by reason of their virulence and intolerance.

A system of government which has a tendency to repel men of high character and position, and attract the needy and unscrupulous, will necessarily be full of corruption. The standard of integrity and honour will be low.[22] And this is what we find in the United States. Posts in the civil service are so many bribes used to win over men whose opposition might prove dangerous. There is a general scramble for the emoluments of office. But this is not the

---

They denounce as copperhead every Republican who offers to differ from them, and exercise really a system of terrorism which has broken down the independent judgment of very many, and makes some of the ablest men in the House and Senate so anxious to avoid their proscription that they are silent, or acquiescent in measures which their judgment condemns."

In the Senate, on the 11th July, 1867, Senator Buckalew made the following remarks:—"If a member of this body gets re-elected, his friends think it is a subject for warm congratulation, regard it as a wonderful result to be wrung from a caucus and from managers at home. But, sir, I insist that in this country, as abroad, the House of Representatives ought to be the great House of our Legislature; its hall should be resorted to for words of eloquence, for profound logic, and for the exhibition of the highest traits of American statesmanship. How is it, and how must it be, as long as you keep members there two, four, and six years only? They have no opportunity to grow up into distinction; they have no opportunity to mature their abilities and become able statesmen."—('Congressional Globe,' 12th July, 1867.)

[22] Burke, in his 'French Revolution,' utters certain truths which seem to have disappeared altogether from modern political discussions, or at best are openly disavowed and repudiated. "Everything," he says, "ought to be open, but not indifferently, to every man." "I do not hesitate to say that the road to eminence and power, from obscure condition, ought not to be made too easy, nor a thing too much of course. If rare merit be the rarest of all rare things, it ought to pass through some sort of probation. The temple of honour ought to be seated on an eminence. If it be opened through virtue, let it be remembered, too, that virtue is never tried but by some difficulty and some struggle."

only, or the worst, form of corruption which exists. Lord Brougham bears this testimony to the honour of the House of Commons:—"I have sat in Parliament for above fifty years, and I never even have heard a surmise against the purity of the members, except in some few cases of private Bills promoted by Joint Stock Companies. I had been considerably upwards of a quarter of a century in Parliament before I ever heard such a thing even whispered; and I am as certain as I am of my own existence, that, during the whole of that period, not one act of a corrupt nature had ever been done by any one member of either House." [23]

The incredulity of a high American official when this passage was once shown to him revealed the difference in the tone of honour which prevails in English and in American public life. Corruption is the first thing to which an American politician of the common order becomes accustomed. He beholds it practised everywhere. It has been brought to bear upon himself, and he is driven to the use of it in his dealings with others. The member of Congress is surrounded with persons who are being bought and sold from morning till night. Before he begins the business of the day, his rooms are besieged by an eager crowd of office-seekers, whose claims, in the larger proportion of cases, he knows to be worthless; but he is bound to advance them. When he goes down to the House he finds himself beset by a

[23] Lord Brougham on the 'British Constitution,' p. 62, chapter iv.

throng of "lobbyists," who haunt the doors of the chamber, and often contrive to follow him upon the floor. Any great interest which is affected by a Bill before the House has active agents at work to make it worth the while of members, such members, that is, as are accessible to gold, to hear and see no more than they are paid to do. If a member is ascertained to have been engaged in a nefarious transaction, it does not injure him in the estimation of his associates, of his constituency, or of the country. This is the worst indication of all of the extent to which public life has been degraded. One instance, among many, may be given in proof of a statement which seems to affect the national idea of probity, although in reality it reaches no further than the political idea. In 1862 a local newspaper in a Western State brought forward accusations seriously affecting the reputation of a member of the House of Representatives. The charge was renewed so often that at last a Committee of the House was appointed to inquire into it. They found that the implicated member was the Chairman of a Committee to which the regulation and disposal of lands in Territories were intrusted, that he had appointed his relatives and friends to posts in all directions, and that he had made a bargain with an agent to buy lands, upon information afforded by the member in question, obtained in his official capacity, and to divide the profits between them. The facts were proved chiefly by the letters of the accused. Once he had written to his underling, "I want to unite with you as a full partner in land speculations and town sites." And again he wrote, by his own admission, "I want to have an interest with you in the city and town lot speculation. The Pacific railroad will go through this Territory, and it will be a fortune to us if I can get it." "I will know all the proposed expenditures in the Territories and post you in *advance*." "I have spent a good deal of time and some money to get this place." The other party to this bargain wrote back saying,—"In the matter of the appointments you may have them your own way; all of them you can save for yourself, and over and above these the partnership matter in land speculations." The facts brought out in the evidence laid open the corrupt intentions of the accused with a conclusiveness which would have been fatal to him in other countries. But there was no proof that any of the transactions agreed upon had really been concluded, and the member was exonerated, and suffered to retain his official position.[24]

In the early part of 1867 the Secretary of the United States Senate, who was the publisher of a public journal, was accused of threatening his party with desertion unless a very lucrative trade contract was made with him. He did not deny the charge, but on the contrary defended it upon principle with great candour. The theory that men should be paid for their political support was, he said, "one that no

[24] For the particulars of this case, see 'Reports of Committees of the House of Representatives,' 1862-63. (Washington, 1863.)

party could discard and live." "Nothing has contributed more to the tremendous and increasing strength of the Republican party than the adherence of such men as Governor —— to the maxim of taking care of their friends."[25] There is no attempt at secrecy or disguise about this. It is not dishonourable for a public official to own that if he upholds his party he expects to be properly paid for the effort. And it is needless to say that the practice is not peculiar to any side or faction; it is the one precedent which all parties defend with perfect unanimity. When the Tariff Bill was before Congress in 1867, and duties on certain articles were enormously increased, statements were openly made in the public papers that interested manufacturers had been busy with their gold among the members. Whether they were well founded or not the mere observer could not decide. They were urged by American journals against American politicians, and they were never contradicted. It is incontestable that the duties most largely enhanced were those upon manufactures, the special representatives of which had seats in Congress. Public writers in America seldom deny that corruption on the most extensive scale exists in the Legislature, unless, perhaps, when the fact is affirmed by a foreigner. The addition of Texas to the Union was notoriously secured by the judicious outlay of ten millions of dollars among members of Congress and

[25] 'Washington Morning Chronicle,' February 14th, 1867.

their friends. Mr. Horace Greeley, no prejudiced witness against his country, says of this great feast—"Corruption, thinly disguised, haunted the purlieus and stalked through the halls of the Capitol; and numbers, hitherto in needy circumstances, suddenly found themselves rich." He adds, indeed, that "this was probably the first instance in which *measures of vital consequence* to the country were carried or defeated in Congress under the direct spur of pecuniary interest;"[26] but the very qualification of the sentence is suggestive. The negotiation is rarely on so colossal a scale, but smaller transactions of precisely the same character are, in the jargon of Congress, constantly "being put through."[27]

---

[26] 'The American Conflict,' pp. 208-9. See also on pp. 209-10 an honest explanation of *log-rolling*, "whereby," says Mr. Greeley, "our statute-books are loaded with acts which subserve no end but to fill the pockets of the few at the expense of the rights or the interests of the many." There are no remarks in the text so full of condemnation as many which might be cited from American writers.

[27] The following is an extract from the New York 'Nation,' a Radical paper, writing of the Radical Legislators for the State of New York:—"A class of bribing agents has sprung up—that is, lobby agents who have laid aside all pretence—to whom the money is confided for distribution, and who do the work as effectually as any other brokers. Nor is the business confined to the corrupt passage of bills. The latest device for raising the wind is the introduction of bills of peculiarly outrageous character, which, if enacted, are sure to ruin a number of persons. It is not intended, however, that they should be enacted. They are merely decoy ducks. They bring the birds to the fowler's net. Numbers of frightened people rush up to Albany, see the legislators, are thoroughly plucked, and sent home somewhat lighter in pocket, but also relieved in mind. The main body of the corrupt drove are lawyers, farmers, and what, not from the interior

The effect of this party rule is, then, to prevent free and fair debate, to destroy independence of opinion, and to introduce into political life men who think it no dishonour to use their opportunities to enrich themselves and their friends. The system in its full and complete working could not possibly produce different consequences. There are, it must again be repeated, many members of Congress who are far above the reach of these discreditable influences. But what we have to ascertain is the *average* kind of politician which the American system brings into existence. That average is unquestionably low. The salary of a member of Congress is often the least of the pecuniary inducements which the position holds out to him.[28] The sentiment of the educated classes is essentially opposed to all that is here described, but the management of public

---

of the State, Republicans in politics, and sound enough on all the great issues of the day to please Thaddeus Stevens himself."—'Nation,' April 11th, 1867.

Another extract from a Radical paper, the 'New York Evening 'Post,' is equally candid:—"In a large proportion of the districts it is expected by the party managers that the men elected to either House will have the opportunity to reimburse themselves for their expenses, and candidates are levied upon accordingly by the party committees, the "strikers" and others. The profession of honourable motives is laughed at. It is expected by the party managers that their creatures will be venal and corrupt, and we have come to that pass, by reason of the enormous mass of special legislation, and the small numbers of the legislature, that bribery is the rule and common practice."

[28] The pay was formerly 3000 dollars a-year, with mileage fees, the privilege of franking, &c. In 1866 it was, by a vote of the members themselves, raised to 5000 dollars a-year.

affairs cannot, but in rare cases, fall into their hands. Energetic local busybodies step in and lead, because honest men dare not engage in the struggle. If every election fairly represented the sense of the industrious and reputable portion of the community, a great change would soon pass over political life. But it is the complaint of Americans themselves that this enviable end is rarely attained.[29] There is no people who have a higher and purer ideal than the Americans; there are none afflicted with public servants who so systematically distort and debase it. The first thing upon which they prided themselves, and the last with which they should have parted, is freedom of discussion. In reality, they are in the habit of encouraging what Mr. Grote calls the "natural tendency of all ruling force, whether in few or in many hands, to perpetuate their own dogmas by proscribing or silencing all heretics and questioners."[30] These words might serve as the description of what takes place in America, whenever the minority attempt a protest against the measures of the ruling party.

---

[29] Mr. Fisher, in his work on the 'Trial of the Constitution,' observes,—"The government is below the mental and moral level, even of the masses. Go among them. Talk to the farmer in his field, the blacksmith at his anvil, the carpenter at his bench—even the American labouring man who works for hire, in the Northern States—and compare their conversation, so full of good sense and sound feeling, with the ignorance, vulgarity, personality, and narrow partizan spirit of an ordinary Congressional debate, and with the disclosures made by investigating committees. Evidently the mind and moral sentiment of the people are not represented."—(p. 347.)

[30] Plato, vol. ii. p. 144.

CHAPTER IX.

THE VOLUNTARY PRINCIPLE IN RELIGION.

THE support of religion is entirely voluntary in the United States. Every sect depends upon its own members for the maintenance of its places of meeting and of its pastors. Religion is self-governing and self-supporting, and there is no denomination which receives assistance from the government, or is even recognised by it. The principle is adopted that the secular government deals with political ends and aims; the church with doctrinal. The functions of the two are kept entirely apart. The utmost licence and freedom are allowed to professors of religion, no matter how extraordinary are the tenets they advocate. The State leaves the Churches to shift for themselves, and the head of the State may go to what church he please, or to none at all, without exciting any remark. Mr. Lincoln was not often seen inside a place of worship, and his successor pays even less attention to public religious observances. The nation feels no interest in the matter. They would no more think of dictating what sect their President should belong to, than they would of ordering the cut of his coat, or prescribing the number of dishes which should be placed upon his table. A man may be as religious or as irreligious as suits his own ideas, without subjecting himself to the least comment or inconvenience.

This freedom from all restraint may be ascribed partly to the effect of a reaction from the extreme stringency practised in past times. The history of ecclesiastical establishments in America proves how slowly and gradually the people became attached to the two great principles of independence and toleration. The early settlers brought out with them the persecuting spirit from which they had themselves suffered so severely. They depended upon carnal weapons for the extension of the spiritual kingdom. The prison, the pillory, and the hangman, were the teachers whose salutary lessons they valued scarcely less than the precepts of their appointed ministers. Every community held that it was the sacred duty of the government to make the profession of religion compulsory, and to visit with the heaviest punishment the indifferent or the backsliding. The colonists had been trained to believe that the assistance of the State was indispensable to the support of the Church, and therefore they insisted upon the imposition of special rates and taxes for that purpose. The voluntary principle was as yet a thing undreamt of. Even had it been proposed it could not have been carried out. The country was not settled, and the population was thin and scattered. The preachers must often have gone without bread if they had been dependent on the chance contributions of their hearers. The State government therefore made provision for them. In New England, a parsonage and glebe of two hundred and fifty acres was commonly given to the pastor. In 1621-22 a law was passed in Virginia levying on every male person of sixteen a tax of ten pounds of tobacco, and one bushel of corn, for the use of the clergy. The expenses of building a church were defrayed by a tax upon the people of a township. The electors decided what description of church they would erect, and how much they would pay a minister to occupy it. At the time of the Confederation, it is estimated that there were eighty ministers in New England, or one to about three hundred of the population. They were all men of education, and at least half of them were graduates of Oxford or Cambridge.[1] These were advantages which gave them weight in the ministry. "The consideration in which some were held," says an American historian, "was the greater on account of their being highly connected."[2] The colonists were not then ashamed of a certain degree of aristocratic feeling, nor had they become avowed levellers of class. And the previous portions of this volume will explain why this was the case. A pure democracy was foreseen by none, and the memorable discovery that laws could render men equal had not been made.

---

[1] Palfrey's 'History of New England,' vol. ii. 38. [2] Ibid.

In those early days the citizen could never forget, and rarely neglect with impunity, his religious duties. He was made pious, or at least to exhibit the external signs of piety, by coercive measures. In Massachusetts and Connecticut no man had a vote who was not member of a church.[3] In Virginia the rights of citizenship were confined to members of the Episcopal Church, and the laws for the propagation of religion were even more rigorous than in Massachusetts. Persons were enjoined to attend divine service every day, and for the third instance of neglect they were liable to the penalty of six months at the galleys. If they missed attending service on Sundays three times, the law ordered the punishment of death.[4] The first laws of the colony punished with death any person speaking against the Trinity, or any article of the Christian faith. Blasphemy was visited with the same penalty.[5] But these merciless laws seemed chiefly designed to frighten the people, for there is no evidence that they were ever put in force. In 1624, however, the Legislature passed a series of laws which were acted upon, the spirit of which may be gathered from the following clause,—"That whosoever should absent himself from divine service any Sunday, without an allowable excuse, should forfeit a pound of tobacco;

---

[3] Baird's 'Religion in America' (New York, 1856), p. 191. Palfrey, i. 345.

[4] Hawkes' 'History of the Protestant Episcopal Church in Virginia,' p. 26.

[5] Baird, p. 180.

and that he who absented himself a month should forfeit fifty pounds of tobacco." Until early in the eighteenth century the laws of the State exacted conformity with the Episcopal Church.

Massachusetts was a hotbed of persecution and intolerance. The political government being exclusively in the hands of church members, they could and did use the civil arm as often as they thought proper in defence of their own opinions, and for the suppression of others. They desired, as their numerous apologists tell us, to preserve their government from corruption, and they acted upon the supposition that elders of churches were proof against ambition and other passions and temptations to which a certain proportion of men in every community are found to yield. It was, says one of the historians, "an aristocracy of goodness" which they wished to establish. It would have been more reasonable to have chosen all their rulers of a certain height, or made the possession of six fingers on each hand the standard of worth. Those would have been requirements which were capable of being brought to a decisive test. But moral excellence defied measurement. The greatest sinner often passed himself off as the holiest man of his neighbourhood. There was no way of proving goodness, and consequently hypocrisy was substituted for it. The prize was worth practising dissimulation to gain, since political power was freely granted to the pious, and those who coveted it had only to affect piety to gain it. It was an easy method of rising to office. And if the offices thus acquired were of no great value in a pecuniary sense, they were by no means unimportant. They gave a man distinction, mark, and power in his own township, and influence over his neighbours. The devout man could soon be put into the shade by the noisy professor. The very mode of admission to the membership of a church, the first condition of political rights, held the door open to lying and all kinds of deception. Candidates were received into the church "upon a relation of their religious experience, or other satisfactory evidence of their Christian character." In many cases this "other" evidence could not, in the nature of things, have been forthcoming. The candidate's own word, his own description of his own goodness, must have been accepted. In such a competition, the fluent and unscrupulous hypocrite would naturally shine out brighter than the halting but earnest believer. It was a contest in which Mr. Worldly Wiseman and Mr. Facing-both-ways had all the favourable conditions on their side. The evil effects of such a system were soon felt. Alarming troubles and dissensions sprung up in the churches, and in 1636 a law was passed intended to have the effect of weeding out the false teachers and professors. The colonists were evidently cast down at the results of their experiment. "Forasmuch," ran their law, "as it hath been found by sad experience, that much trouble and disturbance hath happened both to the church and civil state by the officers and members of some churches, which have been gathered within the limits of this jurisdiction in an undue manner"—therefore it was provided, that no new members should for the future be admitted without the consent of the magistrates and a consultation of the different churches. This was probably the real foundation of that system of ecclesiastical councils or synods, which afterwards became general in New England. The churches met and advised with each other in times of difficulty, or upon troubled questions, without regard to distinctions of sect. They had always done so, but never to the same extent as after they had experienced the difficulty of wisely managing their own affairs. On many occasions these friendly conferences proved the means of healing dangerous breaches and schisms. The meeting "was summoned for a special occasion; it was composed of clerical and lay delegates from such and so many of the neighbouring churches as circumstances made it convenient for the parties interested to convoke; and its existence ceased when the occasion was over. It had no power to act immediately on individual Christians. Its judgment and will, if carried into effect at all, were carried into effect by the individual church or churches to which its counsel was addressed."[6]

The rule of sectarianism gave rise to other evils which were found intolerable as the colony became

[6] Palfrey, ii. 182-83.

larger. The governing men thought they could never be sufficiently oppressive. They tried to kill opinion by killing the individual who professed it. Persons who differed from them were imprisoned or driven into exile, and it was fortunate if a harder fate did not befall them. Superstition and bigotry took the place of reason and law. The errors of the old country were repeated, and even exceeded in the new world. Women were burnt on suspicion of being witches, and, if any one denied the inspiration of the Scriptures, he was first fined and flogged, and then, if impenitent, hanged. In 1651 four Quakers were sent to the scaffold for daring to return to the colony after they had been banished. This sect, indeed, was always visited with peculiar severity. "It is true," says a modern writer, in extenuation of these crimes, that Quakers "behaved in the most fanatical and outrageous manner. Even women among them, forgetting the proprieties and decencies of their sex, ... smeared their faces and ran naked through the streets."[7] These occasional vagaries were a poor justification for all the cruelties heaped upon the harmless Friends. Two women who arrrived from Barbadoes in 1656 were ordered to return immediately, kept in gaol till a ship could take them away, and had their books burnt by the common hangman. Eight others who arrived from England were carried straight from the

[7] Baird, 189.

ship to prison and there detained. Connecticut imposed a fine of five pounds a week upon every town that should "entertain any Quakers, Ranters, Adamites, or such like notorious heretics." Captains of vessels who brought such persons over were obliged to take them back at their own expense, and in Massachusetts they were fined one hundred pounds for every Quaker they landed. In 1656 the General Court of Massachusetts met to enact further proceedings against the "cursed sect of heretics lately risen up in the world, which are commonly called Quakers." It was ordered that every Quaker found in the colony should be sent to gaol, severely whipped, and kept to hard labour and solitary confinement. Several persons soon afterwards suffered the penalties of this law. In 1657 the fine for harbouring Quakers was increased to forty shillings for each hour. Quakers who had once been punished, and were caught in the colony a second time, were to be deprived of an ear; for a third offence they lost the other ear; and for the fourth they had their tongues bored through with a hot iron.[8] Several men and women professing the obnoxious creed were hanged for refusing to leave the colony. At first this treatment made fanatics of many of the persecuted. They walked in procession through the towns clad in ridiculous costumes. Young and chaste women went into congregations stark naked "as a sign."[9] Of

---

[8] Palfrey's 'New England,' ii. 468. [9] Ibid. ii. 483.

one of these persons the chronicler says that this trial of her faith was "exceeding hard to her modest and shamefaced disposition." Deborah Wilson, "a young woman of very modest and retired life, and of sober conversation, as were her parents, walked through Salem naked." Mary Dyer was taken to the gallows (1660), and died saying, "In obedience to the will of the Lord I came, and in his will I abide faithful to the death." A Massachusetts historian of our own day makes a troubled effort to excuse the former rulers of the colony. "The provocations," he says, "which were offered were exceedingly offensive." But he thinks the culprits ought not to have been put to death. "Sooner than that," he exclaims, "it were devoutly to be wished that the annoyed dwellers in Massachusetts had opened their hospitable drawing-rooms to naked women, and suffered their ministers to ascend the pulpits by steps paved with fragments of glass bottles." But they treated the Quakers in a very different spirit, and the stain of their cruelty rests indelibly upon the page of history.

From this glance at the early history of religion in America, it will be seen that the freedom of opinion at present enjoyed has been of very gradual growth. Rhode Island, Pennsylvania, and Maryland, were the first States which did away with religious disabilities and penalties. Rhode Island, indeed, had always extended the fullest licence and liberty to her inhabitants.

When once this toleration was allowed, the Nonconformists spread and multiplied rapidly, and they became so diversified in creed as to render the identification of the State with one particular sect no longer practicable. Which sect should it support? No one could decide. In New England the Episcopal Church was not an object of veneration, for many of the emigrants were Nonconformists who had fled from Europe to escape from her restraints and from her severities. They were not likely to kiss the rod which had smitten them. They brought their religion with them, and demanded the right to practice it unmolested. Men objected to being taxed for the support of any church but their own. What occurred in Virginia affords a perfect example of the mode by which Church and State were separated in America. The Presbyterians became so numerous in the middle of last century that their wishes could no longer be despised. They petitioned the House of Assembly for a redress of their grievances, among which they enumerated their being compelled annually to pay large taxes to support an establishment from which their "consciences and their principles oblige them to dissent." "We ask," they added, "no ecclesiastical establishments for ourselves, neither can we approve of them when granted to others." Memorials to the same effect were presented by other Nonconformist bodies. The adherents of the Established Church endeavoured to protect their interests, and they succeeded in gaining many delays, but the pressure upon them was too constant and too strong to be resisted. In America the majority must have what they ask. The Virginian Legislature in 1776 passed a law removing religious disabilities, and releasing Dissenters from all demands upon them on account of the Episcopal Church. A general assessment for the support of all denominations, the proceeds to be divided equally among them, was afterwards frequently proposed, but never adopted.[10]

In other States, about the same period, the growth of Dissent was equally remarkable. Between 1731 and 1750, a great impetus was given to this movement in the churches by a series of revivals which took place throughout the country. Their success was greatly owing to Whitefield, to whom the people eagerly flocked wherever he went. Large crowds assembled to hear him, day and night. Strong men were struck down suddenly under the power of the word. At Concord he had, in his own words, a "comfortable preaching." The hearers were "sweetly melted down."[11] He tells us that when he preached at Staten Island, the "word fell like a hammer and like a fire." At the beginning of the present century there was another great revival, and a successor

---

10 For the facts here mentioned I have consulted chiefly Dr. Hawkes' 'History of the Virginian Church,' and the 'Records of the Conventions held in Virginia,' to which the Librarian of the Capitol at Washington kindly gave me access. I am indebted to him for many similar facilities.

11 'The Great Awakening,' by Joseph Tracy (Boston, 1842). See pp. 93-97.

to Whitefield, by name Lorenzo Dow, is said to have performed wonderful works therein. At Knoxville, Tennessee, where he preached, "about one hundred and fifty of his hearers were exercised with *the jerks.*" Sometimes the person who received the truth was thrown to the ground by its power, "where he flounced like a live fish."[12] The jerks became an epidemic. Dow writes: "I have passed a meeting-house, where I observed the undergrowth had been cut for a camp meeting, and from fifty to a hundred saplings were left breast-high, on purpose for the people who were jerked to hold on by. I observed, where they had held on, they had kicked up the earth, as a horse stamping flies." "Sometimes," we are further told, the converted ones "cursed and swore and damned."[13] The process of regeneration could not always, it is to be feared, have been an edifying spectacle to the brethren who looked on.

These revivals, wild and ridiculous as some of the incidents which attended them may appear, greatly increased the number of churches of all Nonconformist denominations. Tracy states that one hundred and fifty Congregational churches were formed in less than twenty years. "A considerable number," he says, "of separatist churches were formed, which really added to the strength of the Redeemer's kingdom."[14] At first the abrupt separation from the State was a severe blow to the Episcopal Church,

---

[12] Tracy, p. 222. [13] Ibid. [14] Ibid. p. 390.

especially in Virginia, where it had possessed more attached adherents, and been more prosperous, than in any other part of the country. When the State forsook it, the clergy scarcely knew where to look for the means of living, and many of them returned to England. But that hour of trial was soon over. The followers of the Church rallied to its aid with a single heart and purpose. As the political system of the country gradually produced its natural fruits, the voluntary system in religion became inevitable. Any other would have been impracticable. Where all men are on an equality as regards their political rights, a preference cannot be exhibited by the government for one religious sect rather than another. There is no class with exclusive rights, and to no form of religion can there be given exclusive privileges. Each State in framing its laws adopts the theory which has been described in a few words:—"We consider the primary end of government as a purely temporal end, the protection of the persons and property of men."[15] The Constitutions of the States of Massachusetts, Virginia, and Indiana—a New England, a Southern, and a Western State—may be taken as fair examples of all the rest with respect to this particular subject. They vary in language, not in ideas. Massachusetts guarantees that "no subject shall be hurt, molested, or restrained in his person, liberty, or estate for worshipping God in

[15] **Macaulay**, 'Essay on Church and State.'

the manner and seasons most agreeable to the dictates of his own conscience, or for his religious profession or sentiments." There is a tincture left of the spirit of old enactments in the third clause, which asserts that the people of the commonwealth have a right to invest their Legislature with the authority to require local communities "to make suitable provision, at their own expense, for the institution of the public worship of God," and also to "enjoin" upon "all the subjects an attendance upon the instructions of the public teachers;" but this power is so remotely placed that it could never be exercised. The declaration of rights prefixed to the Constitution of Virginia declares that "all men are equally entitled to the free exercise of religion, according to the dictates of conscience; and that it is the mutual duty of all to practise Christian forbearance, love, and charity towards each other." In this State, as in six others, Ministers of the Gospel are ineligible to sit in either House of Assembly, or to hold political office. The Constitution of Indiana provides that liberty of conscience shall never be restrained by law, and that "no preference shall be given by law to any creed, religious society, or mode of worship; and no man shall be compelled to attend, erect, or support any place of worship, or to maintain any minister against his consent." The Federal Constitution itself distinctly provides that "no religious test shall ever be required as a qualification to any office or public trust under the United States," and by the first amendment, Congress is prohibited from making any law respecting an establishment of religion. Thus, the principle of the government, Federal and State, with regard to religion, is clearly and emphatically expressed. The people are to be left unfettered. Ministers of religion are to live by their calling as best they can, and none of them have anywhere to look for support outside their own congregations.

Let us now endeavour to ascertain whether this system works well or ill. Does religion prosper under it? The statistics of the churches will show that it does, so far as regards its maintenance and support. It is difficult to ascertain the numbers of churches and ministers at the revolutionary period, but the best authorities estimate the former at 1940 and the latter at 1441. "It seems very certain," says Baird, "that in 1775 the total number of Ministers of the Gospel in the United States did not exceed fourteen hundred and forty-one, nor the congregations nineteen hundred and forty."[16] The authorities vary much in regard to the numbers of churches at the present day. Baird, whose book was published in 1856, reckons them at 41,859, of all denominations; while the ministers numbered 29,430, and the members 4,176,431. In a work published in 1854 it is estimated that there were then existing 36,011 church edifices, affording accommodation for

[16] 'Religion in America,' p. 210.

nearly 14,000,000 of persons. This allowed a church for every 646 of the population.[17] In 1866, according to returns published by the respective sects, the Baptists numbered 1,043,641, with 12,675 churches; the Methodists were 1,032,184; and the Episcopalians had 161,224 *communicants*, with 34 dioceses, 44 bishops, and 2530 clergy. Of the clergy it has been stated that "not more than one in six were born and bred in the Episcopal Church. They had been gathered into the fold from all quarters."[18]

These figures make palpable to the eye the progress of religion, so far as the means for its outward observance are concerned. But something more is needed to show the full working of the voluntary principle. Are the churches properly supported? Is it difficult to raise funds for the erection of a place of worship and the support of the pastor? This, of course, depends greatly on the inclination and desires of the community. If they are anxious to have a church, they soon get it. In the older towns, every denomination is usually rich enough to maintain its ministers in comfortable circumstances. But in scantily populated rural districts, or in new settlements, religion starves. The early preachers are little better off than the missionaries to a foreign land. They must share all the hardships and privations of the rude pioneers who have undertaken to

---

[17] *Vide* 'Religious Denominations in the United States,' by Joseph Belcher, D.D. (Philadelphia, 1854).

[18] Sermon by the Bishop of Rhode Island, Sept. 1867.

turn primeval forests into fertile fields. If there are women in the new community, religious worship may be encouraged, but otherwise the strolling preacher, who drops in accidentally, and preaches his sermon, and goes his way after collecting a few dollars, satisfies the settlers. As the ground is cleared, and a village springs up, and the village grows into a town, the agents of religious societies are sent there to begin the organization of a regular church. At first they meet where they can—in a barn, a hut, or a spare room of one of the congregation. Then they put their money together, and perhaps a little help is gained from outside, and a church is built. A schoolhouse soon follows, and in a few years every sect in the settlement has its own meeting-house. Every one helps in the work, each in proportion to his means. As the community grows richer, religion prospers with it. All are satisfied, for all have contributed voluntarily, and can give more or cease to give anything the moment they please.[19]

But the vast majority of these churches, no matter

[19] It is under these circumstances that Minnesota has done so much for the Episcopal Church, owing doubtless to the personal exertions of its indefatigable diocesan, Bishop Whipple.—Some years ago, an English clergyman, the Rev. H. Caswall, saw a church at Buffalo which was being built by the contributions of the congregation. "The ladies had carpeted the church throughout, at a cost of 1000 dollars, and the young men had already raised a fund of 1200 dollars towards the purchase of a peal of bells. The children had furnished the font, and a stained glass window." (See the 'Western World Revisited.') The same thing is done everywhere.

by what name they are called, must necessarily be poor. It is then the Minister or Priest who suffers first, and subsequently the congregation, by the introduction into the priesthood of an inferior order of men. The illiterate will be tempted to enter a profession which they find easy of access, and at least as profitable to them as shoemaking; but the man of education will often shrink back from a career which dooms him to poverty all his days, and shuts out every hope of advancement. He cannot marry, or, if he does, he will often find it no easy matter to win bread for his family. Many men in all countries take up the work of religious instruction with the sole object and ambition of doing good, and it is not to be doubted that there are thousands who cheerfully make this sacrifice of self-interest in the United States. Nevertheless, it is a hard trial for a young man who has been well trained, at Harvard or Yale, and who has lucrative professions open to him, with friends and influence to push him on, to follow the thorny path where he will have to feed upon the crumbs which fall from the tables of his congregation, and walk with many strange companions. Some do it; but many more turn away. "Ministers of the Gospel," said Cotton Mather, "would have a poor time of it, if they must rely on a free contribution of the people for their maintenance." And they have "a poor time of it" as a rule, except in large cities or rich parishes. Very many ministers of the Baptist persuasion receive no salaries at all, and earn a living how they can.[20] The average salary of ministers of all denominations is estimated to be about four hundred dollars a year. The average in the Episcopal Church is three hundred and fifty dollars.[21] The Episcopal Bishop of New York is said to be the highest paid religious functionary in the country, and he receives six thousand dollars a year. "No men among us," says Dr. Belcher, "work harder; no professional men are so poorly paid for their work. Financially, they rank upon an average below school teachers." Sometimes a popular preacher, in a large town, will draw so great a throng of listeners that it is worth while to let the pews by auction, and thus a considerable income is secured. But such cases are rare, and the clergy in nine cases out of ten are badly off. The consequence is that the reservoir of ministers of the Gospel is the poorer class of artisans, and even in flourishing cities men of the rudest education are sometimes found in charge of large congregations.

In many religious bodies the pastor is chosen by the congregation. It is so in the Episcopal Church, but the consent of the Bishop of the diocese is necessary before a clergyman can officiate. The Roman Catholic priests are appointed by their bishops, without reference to the wishes of the congregations. Among the Methodists they are selected at an an-

[20] Baird, p. 276.

[21] Belcher's 'Religious Denominations,' p. 482. Baird, however, estimates their stipend at 600 dollars.

nual conference. The Episcopal Church of America differs from the English chiefly in certain modifications which it has introduced into its forms and ceremonies. The services have been abridged, the Athanasian Creed omitted from the Prayer Book, the marriage and burial services modified, and a number of verbal alterations introduced into the ritual, which seem fastidious rather than necessary or judicious.[22] In the government of the Church each State is made into a separate diocese,[23] and an annual convention is held in every diocese to regulate its affairs. This convention is composed of the clergy, and one or more lay members, who are chosen by the people, or perhaps by the wardens and vestry. The clergy form one

---

[22] The language has been suited to nice ears, and the grammar (as I suppose it is considered) improved. "Those" has invariably been substituted for "them" as a relative pronoun, even in the Lord's Prayer. As an example of the way in which the English has been refined, take the following, from the "Collect for Grace." In the English version the sentence reads: "but that all our doings may be ordered by thy governance to do always that is righteous in thy sight." In the American book it appears thus: "but that all our doings, *being* ordered by thy governance, *may be* righteous in thy sight"—a pedantic schoolmaster's correction. In the prayer for the President (adapted from that for the Queen), "health and *prosperity*" are prayed for instead of "health and *wealth*." But the purist alterations are the most extraordinary. In the *Te Deum* we read: "when thou tookest upon thee to deliver man thou didst *humble thyself to be born of a Virgin*"—the old version not being deemed suitable to polite ears. In the Litany, instead of, "From fornication and all other deadly sin," we read, "From all inordinate and sinful affections." "To dread thee," is changed into "*fear* thee;" "to raise up *them that* fall," into "to raise up *those who* fall;" "so *as* in due time we may enjoy them," into "so *that* in due time," &c.

[23] In New York and Pennsylvania there are two dioceses.

house and the laity another, and a concurrent vote of both is required on any question before any new rule or law can be made. A general convention of all the churches is held once in three years, and in this the Bishops form the upper house, and the clergy and laity the lower. The Church is left free to order its affairs after its own desire, but there is a case in which the Supreme Court of the State of New York interfered to prevent a Bishop deposing a clergyman on the ground of immorality, which had been proved against him. The question, however, with the Court was whether the canons of the Church had been strictly followed, for, if so, it had no jurisdiction. It was decided that there had been no irregularity, and the Bishop removed the clergyman.

It is sometimes asserted that the Roman Catholic Church has extended its authority more rapidly and widely in the United States than any other religious order. But the truth is that its prosperity is maintained only by the constant influx of its followers, in large numbers, from Europe. Roman Catholicism does not take a firm root among the people. The native-born American seldom joins the Church, and the second generation of Irish settlers wander away from it. It is the Irish emigration which sustains it, and consequently it is powerful only in a few of the largest cities on the line of emigration, such as New York and Chicago, Cincinnati and St. Louis. The Archbishops and Bishops are appointed by the Pope, and receive fixed salaries, partly from the cathedral church, partly by an assessment upon the clergy. The priests depend entirely upon voluntary contributions, and fees for marriages and other rites and ceremonies.

Two special merits are claimed for the voluntary over the compulsory system—(1) That a church can be properly supported by voluntary contributions with perfect success, and with no cause of dissatisfaction being given to any; and (2) that the separation of Church and State keeps the Church within its proper sphere, far removed from the dangerous whirlpool of politics. The first of these claims is substantiated by the facts, for, whatever individual ministers may suffer, the Church is constantly extending its influence, and benevolent societies and schools are liberally supported. It has been proved that the Church—any church—can exist very well, can flourish and multiply its followers, without borrowing aid or countenance from the State. But the separation does not keep politics and political influences from reaching religion. De Tocqueville states that the clergy in America "keep aloof from parties and from public affairs."[24] If this was the case when De Tocqueville visited the country, he would be greatly surprised could he revisit it now. It is like his strange remark that "almost all education is intrusted to the clergy,"[25] whereas the clergy have actually far less to do with education than in England. Perhaps in no

---

[24] Chapter xvii. 388.

[25] Ibid.

country in the world is the pulpit used for hustings purposes so systematically, with the general encouragement of public approval, as in America. The Almighty is constantly exhorted to compass the return of the popular candidate, and the misery and discomfiture of his rival. The morning sermon in some churches is a diffuse essay upon the events of the day, in which the Divine approval is announced of certain political opinions. New England preachers address their hearers, in a time of excitement, as if from the stump. The Chaplain in Congress during 1865–67 prayed daily against the President, "that he might be humbled and cast down," and that his own party might be covered with great glory. The best known preacher in America gains his notoriety solely by the freedom with which he discusses on Sunday morning, from a text of Scripture, the acts of public men, and the turn affairs are likely to take. There is probably no good reason why it should not be so; but there is certainly no reason why the fact should be denied. Religion will always influence the course of human affairs, and in America it will interfere in politics all the more energetically because it is not in any way dependent upon the State, but is free to speak openly and without fear of losing its allowance. The preacher accommodates himself to the tastes and wishes of his congregation, and if they demand from him matter which would be more suitable in the columns of the Sunday newspaper, they will have the article, or turn him out and elect another man willing to supply it.

Politics and religion cannot be kept apart. During the rebellion every sect shared in the general disunion, save the Episcopal Church. All through that dark and stormy period, she endeavoured to preserve her children within her fold in the old relations of friendship and love. In the Northern Conventions the names of the Southern bishops were called over, although none answered. The victors, who had not seen their churches burnt to the ground, who had not been forced to stand by helpless while their sacred plate was carried off by a drunken soldiery, and while their registers and papers were destroyed, who had not witnessed the havoc and destruction of all that their congregations held precious—these could easily invite their brethren to be reconciled. But in the South it was different. There, the church and the school, the parsonage and the farm, had alike been pillaged or reduced to ashes. Time-honoured edifices had been riddled with cannot-shot, as at Charleston, or torn to pieces to be made into hospitals and stables, as at Wilmington and other towns, or levelled with the ground, as in Columbia. Sunday after Sunday the congregations came to service with their women in mourning garments and their young men gone. "When my church was set on fire," said an aged clergyman to me, "I took one of my negroes into the vestry and bade him take hold of the plate-chest, while I seized the other handle. We carried it into the street, but some soldiers met us, and one of them slapped me in the face, and abused me, and made me drop it—and

I saw no more of it." Such occurrences could not happen without leaving a deep mark.[26] Many of the Southern clergy held aloof from the Convention of 1865, but the bishops appeared in it, although some desired that the Churches of the North and the South should remain distinct organizations, as they been during the war.[27] But these feelings softened down, and the Churches are united again as of old. Other denominations were long ago torn asunder by sectional political differences. Once, in the words of Calhoun, who thought he saw in religious differences a foreshadowing of general disunion, "all were organised very much upon the principle of our political institutions; beginning with smaller meetings corresponding with the political divisions of the country, their organisations terminated in one great central assemblage, corresponding very much with the character of Congress."[28] But men who hated each other because of political differences, would not meet in friendship just because they were invited to meet in a church.

From what has been said, it will be seen that freedom, equality, and self-maintenance are the principles upon which religious work is carried out in America. In the government of the Episcopal Church the laity have as much influence as the clergy. In nearly all

---

[26] It will be observed that I am not referring to the cause or merits of the war, but merely accounting for the bitter spirit which existed in the minds of Southern clergy (in common with their people) immediately after it was over.

[27] See a letter to the 'Times,' published 31st August, 1855.

[28] Calhoun's speech in the Senate, March 4th, 1850.

other denominations the Church is controlled by the laity. The common theoretical objections which are urged against the voluntary principle are not found impediments in actual practice. "An established church," says Lord Brougham,[29] "enables the government to be administered without any serious obstruction arising from the operation of public feelings excited by spiritual guides." Whereas, the reverse of this, he argues, is the case in America, and moreover he contends that pastors elected by the people can do little good by their ministrations, for the minority will not listen to the man "whose unfitness they have been proclaiming."

It is true, no doubt, that political passions are sometimes fostered in the United States by ministers of religion, but that is an evil not peculiar, or necessarily incidental to, the voluntary principle. The State patronage of religion can never be used as a weapon against the government, whereas in England party or individual preferences or prejudices often originate in the opposition to the alliance of Church and State. The Church makes enemies because it shelters itself behind the political power; the State makes enemies because it singles out one particular church for all its patronage and encouragement. The members of other churches are jealous and aggrieved, and it is easy to stir up in their minds "excited feelings." When the State preserves an impartial attitude towards all sects none

[29] 'Treatise on the British Constitution.

have cause to be jealous of it. When it allies itself with one special sect, that sect alone has a direct interest in supporting it, and all the rest (supposing no other considerations entered in) would be thrown into antagonism. Loyalty and patriotism are sufficient to cast into the shade the question of self-interest, and it is not in England that the established powers have to fear aught from Nonconformists. Lord Brougham says that he dreads the influence of "an all-powerful and wholly independent clergy." Experience in the United States shows how imaginary is such a fear. There the clergy are "wholly independent," but they do not seek to injure the State, from the very motives which make English Dissenters good subjects—the existence of loyalty and patriotism. Lord Brougham's argument implies that the only way to keep the clergy loyal is to fetter their independence, for the moment they are made free they will assail the political fabric. If the State is to have them on its side it must pay them. Such a supposition does more injustice to the Established Church than all the objections and attacks of its opponents. English and American history alike demonstrate the danger of making too close an alliance between religion and the civil power.[30] There have been times when the union of Church and State gave increased power to the *State*, but this was always a disadvantage to the nation. The Church was on the side of despotism and intolerance. Mr. Erskine May

---

[30] See Mr. T. Erskine May's 'Constitutional History,' chapter xii

describes the result when he speaks of Elizabeth's time: "The union of ecclesiastical supremacy with prerogatives already excessive, dangerously enlarged the power of the Crown over the civil and religious liberties of the people." What the alliance of Church and State did in America we have already seen in this chapter.

The objection that, if a congregation elects a pastor, the minority will derive no profit from his preaching, because they were opposed to him, would be too puerile to answer except that it is so gravely made by one who enjoys a high authority. The minority merely preferred another man. Very likely it would turn out that they were better satisfied with the one actually elected. They supported their candidate because they knew him, but his competitor they may not have known. Besides, says Lord Brougham, the people "are little to be trusted with a discretion upon religious subjects." He seems to think that a congregation would change its religious faith and doctrine as often as it changed its pastor. The choice of a minister has nothing to do with the matter. The doctrines are defined and accepted — the question is merely which of two men is most fitting to preach them? In Nonconformist sects in England, that question is decided by election without producing any of the violent consequences which Lord Brougham appears to apprehend. It is the same in America. The pastor is chosen, and the defeated minority would no more think of rising in insubordination than they would of disobeying the laws of the land, because a President whom they did not vote for happened to be the present Executive.

The voluntary system in America works well for the people, but ill, in many cases, for the preacher. Religion itself does not suffer by being placed above the influence of State support and patronage. The State cannot be held responsible for the government of any religious body, it gives offence to none, and the adherents of each sect take a natural pride in doing all in their power to add to its prosperity.

CHAPTER X.

POPULAR EDUCATION.[1]

EVEN Americans who deny that there are any dangers in intrusting the preponderance of power to the bulk of the people, will readily admit that the only safeguard against the growth of future danger consists in the universal spread of education. It is not a question of expediency with them whether they shall educate their poor or not. It is a matter of necessity. They must do it, or submit to the evils attending a rule of men intensely ignorant of the questions they are called upon to decide. The suffrage is open to all, with restrictions in some States which are merely nominal. If men are to govern, they ought at least to be in a position to make themselves moderately acquainted with the course of current events. But the poor are not always willing to send their children to school; they think that it is the duty of their children to help to earn their bread, and therefore the system of compulsory education is recommending itself strongly to the American people.

---

[1] This chapter is partly reprinted, by permission, from the author's letters to the 'Times,' published 6th and 11th July, 1867.

They believe that they have nothing to fear from the exercise of intelligent and educated opinion, and they spare no pains to make provision for the education of all their citizens. After they have done all that lies within their power, they have only partially accomplished their wishes, but they have at least tried to guard against the shame of being practically ruled by men who cannot sign their own names, or read a line of the Constitution.

The duty of providing the means of education is supposed to fall naturally upon the States. So far as this matter is concerned, the State considers itself the head of the family, and sustains the cost of educating those who look up to it for protection. The Federal Government has from time to time allotted valuable grants of land, nominally as loans, among the States for the establishment or assistance of school funds, and a certain proportion of land is always set aside for the same purpose in new States.[2] The charge of the schools is afterwards always borne by each State for itself, and Congress will probably never be able again to lend that liberal assistance which it was always ready to do before the responsibilities of a vast national debt lay upon it. The tax for educational purposes exclusively is now very high in many States—in New York it amounts to 5½ per cent. on the total assessed income,

[2] See for a list of the Enactments of Congress for grants for educational purposes, Kent's 'Commentaries,' vol. ii. pp. 200-201, *note*, Part IV. Lect. xxix.

and in Boston to about half that amount. The people pay it without murmuring, partly because they are proud of the reputation which their country has gained abroad for educating its poor, partly because they perceive that their interests and their duty alike call for the expenditure.

Massachusetts has long held the foremost place in exertions for the cause of education. But the Western States are pressing her hard in the race, and it is generally confessed that the University of Michigan deserves to rank first in the country for the useful and practical character of the training it affords—a training held to be peculiarly adapted to the growth of a Republican country. Chicago has made immense efforts; and these young cities and towns of the West seem determined to outstrip their predecessors in the work of affording instruction to the children of all classes, free of expense. Yet to Massachusetts will always belong the honour of having been the originator of this undertaking. She voluntarily made the necessary sacrifices, and placed upon her own shoulders the inevitable burdens of the task. There never has been a time when she was not ready to acknowledge and meet these obligations. In the earliest days of the Commonwealth the colonists made careful provision for the education of the poor. In 1647 they put into force a definite plan of instruction. They ordered that every township numbering fifty householders should appoint one of its number to teach children, at the expense of their parents or masters; and when the township increased to a hundred households, it was required to set up a grammar school, or pay a fine of five shillings "to ye next schoole till they shall performe this order." From time to time these regulations were enlarged, until they embraced provisions for the support of schools and teachers by all the townships. Wherever the New Englander went to settle, he carried with him the law that out of 63 equal portions into which the chosen territory should be divided, "the first should be for the minister, the second for the ministry, and the third for the school." Thus, as one of the School Committees of recent years states, "the schoolhouse was made the constant companion of the meeting-house wherever these hardy pioneers levelled the forest and set up their humble homestead."

Not until the year 1789 was the basis of the present educational system laid. This was very soon after Washington was made the first President of the Republic, and while the community was still labouring, in poverty and great toil, through the hardest and most trying part of its existence. It would be a long history to recount the details of all the experiments and devices which were tried in order to accomplish the object the people had in view. They attempted many experiments, and found themselves disappointed in not a few. Even to-day they know that their system needs great improvement. But much has been done, and more will yet be done without stopping to count the cost. The people are not immoveably attached to any particular theories, and when they are convinced that a reform is necessary they will adopt it.

The fundamental principle of the present system in Massachusetts is that the authorities must make education compulsory. Children are forced to attend the schools, without regard to the wishes of their parents. There is no choice left either to the pupils or their natural guardians. Officers are appointed to go about the streets and look out for idle or vagrant children, and "compel them to come in." They carry the terrors of the law in their hands. Little by little the penal measures against children who will not go to school have been made more formidable. The opposition to these coercive steps at first was very great. As a superintendent once said to me, "Our people had to be brought up to the idea. They thought that pressure of this kind was not in harmony with a Republican government." I remember that on one of the mornings when I visited the schools the same idea struck a gentleman who was of the party. He was attached to a foreign mission, and seemed startled at finding laws of such a character carried out under a government which asserts itself to be the very embodiment of liberty. "This method," he said to me, a little diffidently, for he was new to the country, "may be a beneficial one in the end to the children, but it is not freedom." I could not forbear telling him that when he had travelled further and seen more, he would dicsover that it was possible in a Republic to place the social life of the people under rules and regulations, and to step into their houses and dictate what they should or should not do, and generally to manage their affairs for them, to an extent which the old despotisms of the world would pause before they attempted.

The compulsory principle is thus set forth by the Superintendent in his report for 1862:—"To secure universal education it is not enough to provide schools at public expense; care must be taken that all children are taught in these schools or elsewhere." In the report of the School Committee for 1847, it is urged that unless the children "are made inmates of our schools many of them will become inmates of our prisons, and it is vastly *more economical* to educate them in the former than to support them in the latter." Here the system is recommended for its economical merit alone; but this is a consideration which has had the least weight with the people, in inducing them to assent to the recommendations made by the school committees.

In order to carry out the compulsory method, a school police force, as it may be called, is indispensable. In Boston this force is small but efficient. The officers arrest children who have never been to schools, or truants, and carry them before a magistrate, who sits privately as a school commissioner, and thus the disgrace and mischief of dragging the juvenile culprits into an open court-room are avoided.

Should the child refuse to attend school, or run away from his teachers a second time, he is sentenced to two years' imprisonment at a Reformatory, which is situated on an island at the mouth of the harbour. I went out to see this institution. It seemed to be conducted with care and attention, but it is to all intents and purposes what it is designed to be—a prison. The children—there were several hundreds there—were dressed in a coarse uniform, and looked like other delinquents in more disgraceful places of punishment. The superintendent assured me that the severity of the punishment "had a very good effect." He meant, of course, that it made parents afraid to refuse to send their children to school, for otherwise they would lose them altogether, under circumstances not usually accounted meritorious or agreeable, for two years.

A member of Parliament in addressing his constituency[3] assured them that the law of compulsory education, even in New England, was a "dead letter," and no one knew enough of the facts to contradict him.[4] It is thus that the government and the institutions of America are conveniently adapted to the views of speculative politicians. One of the truant-officers gives an account of the working of the plan.

---

[3] Mr. Forster, at Bradford, Sept. 1867.

[4] No fewer than seventy-seven towns and cities in New England appointed truant-officers and enforced the compulsory system. (See 'Report of the Board of Education for 1866,' p. 63.)

He says,—"A day seldom passes in which I do not find children out of school. These I send or take into school, hundreds of them every quarter." This is the first step. Another officer describes the second step in the following manner:—

"In cases where I fail to check the habit of truancy and the child becomes an habitual truant, I make a complaint before one of the justices of a police-court; and a warrant is granted me, made returnable at the justice's private room in the Court-house; I arrest the child, and summon the teacher to appear at the time and place named in the warrant. I likewise notify the parents that they may be present and be heard. If the child is found guilty by the Court, a sentence of one or two years in the House of Reformation is passed, and in other instances the cases are continued from time to time in order that the truants may have an opportunity to reform. In these cases they give surety for their appearance at the time specified by the Court. If they are sentenced, I take them directly from the Court to the steamer 'Henry Morrison,' and leave them in charge of the officer of the boat, who delivers them into the custody of the officers of the House of Reformation at Deer Island."

One of these scholastic policemen—not an unimportant officer in the work of education—tells us that he had charge of 1191 cases during a single year (1862), recorded the names of 321 truants, and obtained proof of 2091 truancies. This was the record of one district only in the city of Boston.[5] There is a general law in the State of Massachusetts under which similar proceedings might be taken everywhere, but it is at the discretion of each town whether it shall be put in force or not. In most communities it is left to lie idle, principally on account of the expense involved in its rigorous execution. A special corps of inspectors has to be paid, and a separate place of punishment built, before such a law can be carried into effect. That education is so generally diffused in Boston need not, then, be a subject of astonishment.

The city deserves the greatest credit for the sacrifices it constantly makes to support its schools, but it is not to the credit of the poor that they send their children to them. They dare not send them anywhere else. Prevent parents from despatching their boys or girls to work, and force them instead to support them while at school, and the first and greatest obstacle to the education of the very poor—namely, the impossibility of securing the regular attendance of the pupils—is disposed of at a stroke. The end doubtless justifies the means, but the Boston process scarcely recommended itself formerly to nations which, although living under "tyrannical monarchies" and "cruel despotisms," were accustomed to consider their children their own, and their homes sacred.

The arrangement of the schools is the same in

[5] According to the Annual Report of 1866, the total number of truant cases in ten years was 2741.

essential particulars in all the States, but it is seen to the greatest advantage in Boston, and hence I select that city for the purpose of illustration. There the schools are divided into three grades—the primary, grammar, and high schools. Children are admitted to the primary schools upon the sole condition that they present a certificate of vaccination, and thereafter there is no fee or charge required from them. They are taught from books specially prepared or sanctioned by the committees, and there is an inspector appointed whose duty it is to see that a settled plan of tuition is not departed from. To the teachers there is left no liberty of judgment. They suggest nothing, alter nothing; they are merely employed to keep in motion certain wheels which are turning in all the schools in the same direction at the same hour. The buildings are laid out and erected upon one design, and the work which goes on inside knows no variation. No doubt it is unavoidable, perhaps it is desirable, that this uniformity should be insisted on; but if there are imperfections in the general method the universal application of it must be productive of some undesirable consequences. It is the boast that all classes may be educated together, but there are not a few who allege that the plan does not work so well as it ought to work, and that the "course" is better adapted to the children of the rich than the children of the poor, and cannot possibly be perfectly adapted to both. Nevertheless, all may be benefited by the system to the extent that they may learn to read and write, and work common sums in arithmetic. And in some cases the children of the very poorest parents may be found at the head of the school, and the circumstance would happen oftener, but that the tolerably well-to-do can alone afford to keep their sons at school during the period required to complete the studies assigned to higher grades. At the age of five years the pupil enters the primary school, where he is taught the alphabet, and the first rudiments of knowledge, advancing one grade each half-year. These elementary schools appear to be less open to objection than any of the more advanced. Teaching the alphabet and a little writing and arithmetic give no scope for the introduction of crotchets, or the exercise of painful ingenuity. The children seem to have their tasks duly measured to their capacities, and in most instances they make remarkable progress. They are not overworked, and they are not allowed to take their lessons home with them. They go to school in school-hours only. The teachers are chiefly women—there being attached to all the schools in Boston 547 female to 66 male teachers. From the very outset, the greatest attention is paid to the physical development of the pupils. At intervals during the day they go through a series of muscular and vocal exercises, which are intended at once to relieve the tedium of school-hours, and preserve the health of the scholars. They are taught to throw out their arms, to draw them back again suddenly, to raise them aloft, to bend them back—accompanying each motion with the letter of a word they are set to spell, or some similar exercise. The managers pride themselves much on this muscular tuition, and the pupils (except those whose physical weakness renders the amusement a hardship) seem to take delight in this interruption of their desk-work. They are also required to practise certain eccentric exercises for strengthening the vocal organs; and this portion of the system is carried out with a vigour which is more confusing than instructive to the visitor. In the first schools music is taught by a simple and excellent method—so simple that, after a little practice, a boy or girl, five or six years old, is able to teach all the others.

After three years of this elementary training, the pupil is supposed to be ready to pass to the grammar school, where he is required to apply himself to severer studies. The advanced schools are of various merit, but the teachers are generally chosen with care and discrimination. Five or six years must pass before the pupil can be ready for the last stage, the high school, and there, too, he must remain some years before he is turned out the finished product of New England education.

The scheme thus sketched forth is objected to on numerous grounds. The education given is not, it is contended, of a sufficiently practical or useful character. "Our schools," says an American writer, "instead of discharging their advanced pupils fitted for embarking in the practical and useful careers of life, send them out into the world filled with a crowd of vague ideas, potent discontents, and restless desires." In other words, the writer believes that the pupils receive an education not only above their station, but one which unfits them for it and makes them miserable in it. "It is now the common complaint," he says, "that our youth are unwilling to apprentice themselves to the industrious arts. The supply of skilled workmen in almost every branch of trade is daily becoming less; . . . . the sons of our better mechanics are all aspiring to become merchants or professional men." But this is not a defect of any educational system in particular; it is an argument which could be urged against education itself, although with great impropriety and shortsightedness. To educate the people is a good work, and, if it leads them to strive to rise beyond their station, their disappointment or their success will be its own answer to their ambition. The same writer proceeds to make a remark respecting the effect of the common school education upon the national character:—"The characteristic of our American community is a liberal diffusion of ideas accompanied with a very little accurate knowledge, of which our excessively illogical legislation is both the proof and the consequence." It will be observed that this, again, is a very different picture of the state of society in America from that which is constantly drawn by a section of politicians in England.

It is complained, moreover, by the Americans themselves, that the effect of the present educational system is to benefit the rich at the expense of the poor. Wealthy families can afford to let their children remain long enough in the schools to pass through all the grades; poor people cannot. They are obliged to take their children away before they have derived much benefit from the schools. The report of the School Committee for 1866 practically admits this defect, without acknowledging that it is an evil:—"Many pupils never see the interior of high schools; others who enter the high schools leave them before they have concluded the proper course." And in another report it is stated, as a subject for congratulation and a proof of the success of the schools, that—"The proportion of the children of our citizens now educated in them is as twenty to one over those educated at private expense. Why should it not become a matter of honest ambition among families of the amplest means and truest judgment, to have their sons and daughters here educated; the children of the mechanic and the merchant sitting side by side, pleasant companions in youth, as they will be sympathizers and helpmates through the remainder of the journey of life?"

This beatific picture naturally charms a people which pays no honour to station or degree, and which is accustomed to rejoice in its contemptuous disregard of even intellectual distinctions; but it misses the real point of the objection. The charge is that the course is intended for the rich, and is practically beyond the reach of the poor. To amend this fault, greater care should be bestowed upon the first three years of tuition. The course is both ambitious and elaborate, but it is also too pretentious to be well adapted to the ends in view. It is too extensive and too difficult for popular education. This pretentiousness exhibits itself in various ways in the work of every class—notably, as it often seemed to me, in the way the pupils are taught to read. They declaim with an artificial inflection, tone, and manner, not ill adapted to the exercises prepared for them in the books, which largely consist of ornate speeches or poems, but totally incompatible with the ordinary sense of pleasure derived from hearing a book well read. I heard several young ladies recite poems or speeches; and although it may have been a very grand and powerful style which they adopted, especially if they were designed for a public career, it seemed to my ear very stilted, absurd, and even distressing. Nothing can be more objectionable than to hear young girls or boys mouthing and ranting like strolling players in a barn. As I went up the stairs of the Girls' Normal School one day, and heard the pupils reading together, I could not but think how much those of them who were born with common sense and good taste would censure their injudicious preceptors in years to come. "We have done away with the regular school drawl and drone," I was told; but this very harmless defect was not improved by the vice which was substituted in its place.[6]

During the past twelve years the authorities have raised by taxation, and spent in educational purposes, nearly 7,000,000 dollars. They have now under their control 280 schools, in which the average number of pupils in 1866 was 27,723. The expenses of the schools for that one year amounted to nearly 800,000 dollars, or an average cost per scholar of 20·77 dollars. The pay of the teachers is as low as it can well be, averaging less than 55 dollars a month for males, and less than 22 dollars for females. The frequent complaints of the inadequacy of this remuneration are, perhaps, the best founded of all those which are brought against the Massachusetts

---

[6] The school-books give directions for "reading with taste," which are well calculated to distract the pupil, or ruin any natural taste he or she may have. They are told when to use a "slide," and passages are printed for their guidance, so that they cannot make a mistake. The following is an example :—

Examples of the "subdued or pathetic" kind for "soft" standard force.

1. "Little Nell was *dead*. No *sleep* so *beautiful* and *calm*, so *free* from trace of *pain*, so *fair* to look upon. She seemed a creature FRESH from the hand of GOD, and *waiting* for the *breath* of *life*; not one who HAD *lived* and *suffered* DEATH. Her *couch* was dressed with here and there some *winter-berries* and *green leaves*, gathered in a spot she had been used to *favor*. 'When I *die*, put *near* me something that has *loved* the LIGHT, and had the SKY *above it always*.' Those were her words."

The affected and unnatural manner in which the pupils—especially the girls—read such passages as these defies description.

system, for they result in deterring competent persons from joining in the work of teaching, and fill the schools with incapable or empirical "professors." Hence it is that the quality of the education which a boy of ordinary capacities receives is so low and bad. The sharp boy is picked out, and well crammed, and kept for exhibition to visitors. The rank and file get through their daily tasks, or leave them undone, and there is no inducement for the teacher to push them forward.

It is obviously of the utmost importance to the American people that they should not be misled or deceived, by their agents or servants, in this great work of educating the young. An obligation lies upon them to employ the most efficient instruments they can find, not to sacrifice the object they have in view for the sake of accommodating the caprices and vagaries of a few men, who have no stronger claim to manage public instruction than that they think they understand the subject better than any one else. It is admitted now that most of the ideas originally adopted in the Massachusetts schools were wrong. In a few years' time the successors of the present committees, trustees, and inspectors may pronounce the same judgment on the experiments which are now being tried.

The work of education in the United States is, in fact, entirely an experimental one down to this very hour. Mistakes and defects in it are constantly being discovered and pointed out, even by those who have the greatest interest in being blind to them. Old details of the plan are constantly being discarded, and new theories attempted in their place. The national anxiety for the education of the young, however, always remains, and it is this which gives the true direction to the officers who are placed in charge of the schools. Education in a democratic community is as necessary as the standing army which its internal differences call into existence. Much credit is doubtless due to the charitable intentions of the community, but the prevailing motives for the sacrifices they make are those of protection for themselves, and regard for the destinies of their country. It is of little consequence, the American believes, how many people you admit to the suffrage so long as you can rely upon their all voting intelligently, upon proper reflection and information. To enfranchise large numbers of persons who have not proved themselves to be qualified to form rational opinions upon public affairs, and whose antecedents are a presumptive evidence of their unfitness to be intrusted with a share of political power, is an act which, even in a democracy, excites discontent and many misgivings. This is proved by the strong and general opposition which exists in the United States to negro suffrage—an opposition so strong, that the people who insist upon its acceptance by one section of the country refuse altogether to hear of its enforcement in their own. It was required that the South should let negroes vote, not because any one believed or pretended that the negro was qualified to vote intelligently; that was never asserted; but because the concession was regarded as a just compensation to the race for the hardships and sufferings inflicted upon them in previous generations, as a security for their freedom, and as a measure of retaliation against those who endeavoured to divide the Republic—in short, upon a variety of political considerations which are wholly independent of the propriety or impropriety of allowing uneducated persons to take a direct share in the government. If the question of negro suffrage had been decided upon the latter basis alone, the whole voice of the country would have been raised against it. Expediency, political conceptions of justice, party spirit, were the motives, and the only motives, which led the country to sustain it.

"The people must be educated before they can safely be intrusted with political power," is, then, a ruling maxim of every American who has a true knowledge of the principles of his own government, or a just appreciation of others. During the political contests which followed upon the termination of the war, the most intensely radical section of New Englanders were exceedingly solicitous respecting the education of former slaves. They knew perfectly well that, if these ignorant blacks were allowed to govern, fresh as they came from the cotton-field and the sugar-brake, great and wide spread must be the mischief which would ensue. Hence the demand arose for confiscation of Southern lands, for the purpose of creating funds wherewith to found and endow schools. Of so much consequence is it held to be that all persons shall possess facilities for forming independent opinions upon the course of public affairs, that in Massachusetts every man must be able to read and write before he is allowed to cast his ballot. Supposing that Massachusetts citizens held that it was equally necessary in the South to adopt this safeguard and protection, it would follow that the negro could not vote. But other considerations determined the question, and the instant admission to political privileges of four millions of scarcely civilized voters, was thought to be the least of the two evils between which the nation saw itself compelled to choose.

The voluntary principle in religion has also had its influence in encouraging free education. Each sect was not only obliged to build its own churches and support its own priests or clergy, but also to take proper measures for the education of the young. These denominational institutions now exist all over the country, and greatly limit the scope of the purely secular schools. An inspector of the public schools once complained to me, "every denomination thinks it must have its own school, and hence our field is sadly reduced." The eighth census shows us that nearly five millions of persons received instruction in the various States in the year 1860; but this return included schools of all descriptions. The schoolhouse always springs up, as if in a night, by the side of a church. In a new settlement the one is never considered complete without the other. They are nourished with an equal hand, and thrive commensurately with the growth of the community. The poorest cheerfully give of their slender substance to protect the welfare of their sect, which to their minds is advancing the great cause of religion, and to provide means for the instruction of the young. The secular principle in education is indispensable, where the chief object aimed at is to entice parents of all shades of religious opinions to send their children to school. It is, therefore, an essential and not an optional part of the educational system in America. Indeed, the managers of these institutions sometimes strive too hard, and sacrifice too much, to make their establishments popular with all. They offend many by their over anxiety to keep religion outside in the street, and to "conciliate" certain sects. When one of the schools in Boston was opened, the usual devotional exercises were abridged, and the reading of the Bible altogether omitted, because the building was in the midst of a Roman Catholic population, and several priests had been invited to attend. This pleased the Catholics very much, it was said, and probably with truth; but Massachusetts has always been a Protestant community, and it is possible to avoid giving offence to Roman Catholics without tricking out the schools in false colours and disguises to accommodate them to their dogmas.

If all the appliances for education in America were excellent of their kind, the children of Americans ought to be the best educated in the world; but will any one except a very prejudiced and uninformed observer assert that they are so? The effects of a superficial and desultory training are palpable to every one who lives in the country, and who watches life and manners with impartial eyes, and who has listened to the frequent complaints of parents that their sons know nothing thoroughly. "They skim over the surface of things," it will often be said, "and will not work, as one reads and hears of English boys doing." There is no people in the world who read so much and know so little as the Americans. It will be understood that this remark applies simply to the masses, who live upon a mental diet furnished by newspapers, and cheap magazines, and tawdry novels. The learned class are by no means few in number, and it is yearly strengthened by the sound and efficient work done in the excellent Universities of Yale and Harvard. There, some of the finest intellects in the country have been cultivated, and men of distinguished abilities daily conduct the studies of the graduates. It is not the fault of any of the States within the Union if their inhabitants are not possessed of a common and serviceable education. They appreciate the truth of the words pronounced by Mr. Robert Lowe, in the House of Commons, "that it is absolutely necessary that their masters should be taught their letters." While England is intent upon imitating the elective franchise of the United States, she must also borrow from the Americans their ideas upon education, and make schools at least as numerous as polling-booths, or she may find that she has imported from another nation a recognised element of disturbance, without also providing herself with the only security which it was within her power to obtain

CHAPTER XI.

CAPITAL AND LABOUR.—RELATIONS BETWEEN EMPLOYER AND EMPLOYED.

It is sometimes asserted by speakers and writers whose claims to authority justify us in expecting an average degree of accuracy in their statements, that there is no dissatisfaction among the working classes of America, that every man is sure of being properly paid for his labour, that class distinctions do not exist, and that combinations of labour against capital, or of capital against labour, are impossible. Trades' Unions, we are told, are unknown, and "such a combination of class against class as that with which we are afflicted [in England] would be an absurdity, when all alike are in possession of political power, and at liberty to promote and defend their own interests by constitutional means."[1]

These representations are probably not intended to convey the truth about America, so much as to serve

[1] See an essay by Mr. Goldwin Smith, in 'Essays on Reform' (Lond. 1867). Compare his confident statements with the following from a high American and *Radical* authority, the 'North American Review,' for July, 1867 (p. 178):—"Trades' Unions have, in many of the great branches of industry here, been brought to as high a degree of efficiency as in Europe."

certain party purposes in England. On no other ground can their extraordinary incorrectness be explained. In America there is a wealthy class, and there is also a poor and a discontented class. The rich are sometimes selfish, and the privations of the poor are embittered by the sense of injustice. These circumstances are even now common in the United States, and as the manufacturing population increases they will become still more common. The labour question is a subject of trouble and anxiety to thoughtful men in the United States, and it is complicated by the fact that in the political government economic laws are neglected or misunderstood. One cause of this, as a recent American writer justly points out, "has been the wonderful material prosperity of the country. . . . . The abundance of land rendered the existence of a poor labouring class almost impossible, until the great factories came into existence."[2] No honest and well-informed writer would attempt to deny that the "labour question" in the United States is one of the most serious before the country. But it cannot become a great social canker while the discontented poor can be silenced by the advice, "Go out West," where employment of some sort can be obtained by men able and willing to work hard.

Perfect extinction of class feeling may possibly be an unattainable blessing, but certain it is that the

---

[2] 'The Nation,' Sept. 26th, 1867.

time-worn troubles and dissensions are revived in America, with this difference, that there the labouring classes have the balance of political power on their side. Trades' Unions, strikes, outrages upon employers or independent workmen, are nowhere more common than in the United States, and the working classes are sometimes inaccessible to a sense of justice and fair dealing, through the conviction that the controlling influence in the machinery of government rests with them. The workmen, whenever they determine upon a strike, or disagreee with their employers from any cause, almost invariably find the public men and the press upon their side, or at least no more opposed to them than is implied in the proffering of some very good advice. The reason is plain. The employers do not form a class worth taking any trouble to conciliate, for when they are counted by heads they are of less importance than the employed; and they have no political power or interest except that which, in rare and exceptional cases, they derive from the support of the labouring class. The employer is powerful only when the employed act in unison with him. If he is opposed to them he can do nothing. For example, certain wealthy manufacturers have contrived by various means to convince the working classes that a Protectionist policy is indispensable to their welfare. "Unless your work is protected," they tell them, "it will be impossible to pay you good wages, or even to give you regular employment, because other countries will step in with their goods, and we cannot stand against their competition. Therefore you must insist upon prohibitory duties for foreign merchandise, and by that means you will be able to keep what is your own." With the exception of the Democratic party—of course an important exception—all classes in the country are deceived by these fallacies, long ago exploded in England. The workmen believe in them, and support a protective policy, and thus the manufacturers are able to pass tariff bills which are the wonder of the world, and which fill their own pockets at the expense of the general community.

But let true ideas concerning political economy once reach the working classes—an end difficult to accomplish, because their reading is chiefly confined to the newspapers of their own party, where they only see reproduced with eternal sameness the old objections to free trade—and there would be no power left strong enough to keep a Protectionist policy in operation. The employers could not do it, for they have no more weight in the country than an equal number of their workpeople. They have the means of buying support, it is true, and in all alarming dangers which menace them they know how to employ this resource with success. The lobbies of the State Legislatures and of Congress are often the scenes where the real battle between labour and capital is fought.[3] But this refuge cannot be

[3] Sufficient has been said in previous chapters with reference to the corruption existing in the country, but an extract from a memorial presented by the "Citizens' Association" of New York, and signed by

available in every emergency. When combinations of Trades' Unions demand an advance of wages which the masters will not concede, they strike, and the victory depends, as it does everywhere else, upon the relative powers of endurance of each side. But in America the men on strike find themselves the object of the sympathy and encouragement of the politicians. In the spring of 1867 there was a clamour in many of the Northern States for a law to render eight hours' work a legal day. In the West it was vigorously resisted by the masters, and as they spared no efforts to introduce fresh hands from abroad, they gained the day. But in New York the Legislature gave way to the pressure without a scruple, and passed the eight hours' law. No one could say that this was a just or a fair measure, for why should an employer be compelled to pay the same price for eight hours' work which he formerly paid for ten, at the very time when men are willing to work ten hours, but are forbidden by the arbitrary rules of Trades'

Mr. Peter Cooper, a well-known inhabitant of that city, may be given here :—

"It is well known to every intelligent man conversant with public affairs, that corruption has become organized throughout our State, and has assumed such alarming proportions that capital, labour, and the industrial and commercial classes are oppressed to a degree unknown even in countries where the most absolute and tyrannical form of government prevails.

"The demoralizing influences of corruption are rapidly penetrating social life, and tampering with the Press, the Pulpit, and with the Judge upon the bench, poisoning justice at the fountain-head, sapping morals, religion, and education."

This memorial is dated Sept. 13th, 1867.

Unions? Of course the masters protected themselves by paying their men by the hour instead of the day; no law could prevent that. In April, 1867, there were no fewer than twenty trades on strike in the States of New York, New Jersey, and Pennsylvania, and the men were all paid weekly contributions from Trades' Unions. As the town and city populations extend, the difficulties between labour and capital will become more serious, for the idea of universal equality is held to be inconsistent with one man dining on half a loaf, while another rides by in his carriage. It is easy to convince men who have the balance of power on their side that the existence of a wealthy class is a great social wrong. There can be no greater fallacy than to assert that combinations of class against class are impossible in America, because "all alike are in possession of political power, and are at liberty to promote and defend their own interests by constitutional means." All are not in possession of political power alike. The great weight of power falls to the share of the working classes, and American employers know that only in mockery or in ignorance could the statement be made of them that they are removed from the fear of injustice, because they can defend their interests by "constitutional means." They are outnumbered. The labouring classes in America are often dissatisfied, but, as they cannot ascribe their wrongs to the tyranny of the rich, or to an aristocratic government, and as the labour-market is more at their command than working men find it in England, their discontent seldom spreads into a wide agitation. They think they are underpaid, as working men do in England, but they cannot allege that all would be righted if they were admitted to the franchise. The bulk of them know that they cannot escape from the necessities of a life of toil. No one can mount to power on their shoulders by magnifying their political grievances, or win their sympathies by telling them that a vote will be a remedy for all their troubles, and then undertaking to procure for them that vote. A variety of the same species of demagogue finds, however, ample field for his work. He goes about inciting the employed against their employers, and that golden dream of the idle and worthless, a "redistribution of property," is now and then held out to dazzle them. In the summer of 1867, no less an authority than the President of the United States Senate, a leader of the Republican party, made a journey westward, in the course of which he delivered several speeches upon the labour question. He distinctly told his audiences that capital had accumulated too much in a few hands, that the day was coming when that arrangement must be disturbed, that Congress, which had done so much for the slave, could not leave the working man uncared for, and that God never intended a man to labour all his life.[4] In every form of society there are thou-

[4] Mr. Wade, the official in question, never repudiated the sentiments conveyed in these words, although his friends, when they saw

sands of persons in whose ears words like these would be music. Give them first the desire to possess their neighbour's property, and then the power, and how many of them would hesitate to take it because it did not belong to them? The security against the gigantic wrong suggested by the President of the Senate is in the number of small proprietors scattered over the country; but the surplus populations of the cities are fast growing, and all power is in the hands of the multitude. Unfortunately for mankind, it is a mistake to suppose that in the American government there are provisions for reconciling all interests and satisfying all desires—that in the United States one class never can lift its hand against another class, because all are equal in the government, and a special wrong can fall upon none.

The true sentiment of the working classes in America may be judged of from their own written statements or speeches. In Chicago, in the early part of 1867, a journal was established by some working men for the advocacy of their rights. In a preliminary manifesto the following principles were laid down:—"Mankind is an Universal Brotherhood." "Association is the first principle of economy." "Union is strength; isolation is weakness." "*There*

---

the ill effect they caused, denied that he had said what was attributed to him. But the editor of the 'New York Times,' a gentleman of high repute and character, made careful inquiries, and assured the public that the report he had published was entirely accurate. Moreover, several persons present at the meeting testified to the reporter's fidelity.

are no rights but the rights of Labour."[5] At a meeting of workmen held in Chicago,[6] a member of Congress[7] said that capital and labour never did or can unite," and he added—"Capital *must not be allowed* to be centralized in the hands of a few." These declarations were received with immense applause, and the following seemed to give equal satisfaction:—"If the labouring men produce the wealth, they must control it; and if all the working men agree upon this, their success is certain." A General of the army[8] told the meeting that they could make what laws they pleased, and therefore they need not long be oppressed. The President himself sent a letter to the men—who were out on strike—in which he assured them of his sympathy and good wishes. Thus petted and flattered, it would be strange if the working classes always preserved a calm judgment, or were always guided by a sense of fairness.

Not only are strikes frequent in America, but they are attended by all the disgraceful circumstances which mark the worst combinations of the kind in other countries. Still to refer to a single year, in May, 1867, there were several incendiary fires in St. Louis and Chicago, after "mass meetings" of the working classes. In the eastern district of Pennsylvania, a mining region, the men killed fifty agents

---

[5] See the 'New York Tribune,' of March and April, 1867.

[6] In May, 1867. An account of it may be found in all the leading American papers of the time.

[7] Mr. Kuykendall of Illinois.

[8] General Wallace.

or miners in the space of four years. "When criminals are arrested," said a local record,[9] "no testimony can be had. The case was related of a man walking out with his wife. He was shot by her side, and, although as many as fifty persons were standing by, no proof could be obtained." It is generally said, when such crimes are revealed, that the perpetrators are foreigners. But this is surely no proof that the perfection of government is found in the United States. It only shows that, whatever may be the defects of the English form of government, it is not to them that the discontent of the labouring classes can be traced, since that class is just as discontented in America where there is nothing to complain of, and adopts precisely the same method of making its discontent known and felt. If it be political oppression which gives rise to the alleged wrongs and sufferings of the working man in England, he ought to be relieved from them directly he takes up his abode in a land where there is no political oppression, except such as his own class originates. But this is the very class, according to Americans, which commits all the outrages, and causes all the disturbances, in their country; and thus they afford involuntary proof that their "free institutions" have nothing to do with the success of the government, but that it is due to the superfluity of land, and the immense natural resources of the

---

[9] 'New York Tribune,' letter dated, "Pottsville, April 14th, 1867."

Republic. The relations between capital and labour can probably never be better dealt with than when they are left to regulate themselves, without the interference of the Legislature. One side or other is sure to be dissatisfied with the mediator, if he is armed with the power of enforcing his decision. It may be said with truth that in America nothing has yet been done towards settling the great social problem which has embarrassed older communities for generations past. There conditions exist which ought to ensure, if anything could, a perfect understanding and entire harmony between employer and employed—a boundless market, land to be had almost for the asking, abundance o room for all. Yet even in a country so blessed we find most of the melancholy antagonisms and feuds of the Old World faithfully reproduced. Is it any wonder that perfection is not attained in a land where neither of the advantages just enumerated can be enjoyed, where labour and capital are encumbered by a thousand difficulties which cannot be experienced across the Atlantic in the present century? A large pauper population and an overburdened market, almost every trade so crowded with competitors that a low rate of wages is a natural consequence,—these are the disadvantages under which an old community labours. Many earnest men of America still hope to satisfy the expectations of the emigrants who flock to their shores from all parts of the world by gradually bringing into general custom the plan of co-operative workshops and association. Several establishments based on this principle have already been tried in the West. In New York the experiment has failed. But the scheme is still regarded with confidence, and the idea of the "progressive" party is that there shall be no more hired labourers in the country, but that men shall work for a share of profits instead of for wages.[10] These aims can be accomplished in the United States, if anywhere. Almost any experiment can be attempted there with safety. But the good is all to be achieved in the future, for at present the working man, without capital to assist him, is scarcely any better off in America than he is in England, and a skilled workmen is not often so well off. He is taxed as heavily as in England, if the price he is compelled to pay for clothing be taken into account, and his wages are only nominally higher. The dollar in these days is not more than the equivalent of the English shilling. The addition of that modern specific for all human troubles, the "vote," is not always sufficient to compensate the workman for the inconvenience of uprooting his old associations, and for the expense of settling his family in a strange land.

---

[10] See the 'North American Review,' for July, 1867.

CHAPTER XII.

PROSPECTS OF THE UNION.

We have seen that at every stage in the history of the Union a large proportion of the people have been profoundly dissatisfied with the government, and that even the founders of the Constitution seriously questioned its stability. In three States only was the Constitution adopted unanimously, and in other States there was scarcely a sufficient majority to carry the measure.[1] The Convention in which the instrument was drawn up several times nearly separated without coming to any agreement. Washington admitted that the contest had been one, not so much for glory, as for existence. John Quincy Adams[2] spoke of the Constitution as a compact "extorted from the grinding necessity of a reluctant nation." It had no sooner been ratified than it brought into existence two great parties, which have ever since, under various names, been at issue concerning the construction of its fundamental provisions. The interests of the States were incompatible, and their bitter dissensions have deepened with

[1] Story, chapter ii. p. 191. [2] Sixth President.

each successive generation. In a very remarkable letter from Jefferson to the ex-President Martin Van Buren,[3] he says—"General Washington was himself sincerely a friend to the republican principles of our Constitution. His faith, perhaps, in its *duration* might not have been as confident as mine; but he repeatedly declared to me that he was determined it should have a fair chance of success." Hamilton, it is well known, thought that the government could not last; and men like Otis, Hopkins, John Adams, and Gouverneur Morris—all of whom had an important share in defining the Constitution—fully agreed with him. Two years before Hamilton's death—namely, in 1802—he wrote a letter to Gouverneur Morris, in which he spoke of himself as "still labouring to prop the frail and worthless fabric."[4] By more than one great American it has been held that the founders of the Constitution intended to provide the means for bringing the government to a peaceable end, by the failure of choice of electors.[5] Others anticipated dismemberment from the increasing area of the Union, and from the impossibility of establishing a complete identity of feeling or interests.[6] With the growth and prosperity of the country,

---

[3] Written 29th June, 1824, and first published in 1867. See 'Political Parties,' by Martin Van Buren (New York, 1867). Appendix, p. 434.

[4] Ibid. p. 84.

[5] Ibid. p. 48, and *supra*, p. 58.

[6] "This country, fully peopled or half-peopled, is large enough to make five or six great nations, each with its system of central and local government. The time will come when it will be so divided,

unforeseen sources of danger have arisen. That new and vast community which is growing up on the Pacific coast may not always be contented to endure the restraints of the Federal bond, and may insist on casting it off. Except in their attachment to the national idea, the Union has little hold upon the Pacific States. Indeed, the most potent cause of disaffection, and the one which is ever at work, is the want of strong political sympathy between the people North and South, East and West. The determination of the North to extinguish the individualism of the South, and of the East to perpetuate a policy of prohibitory tariffs and protection, so fatal to the interests of the West, are far from being the only instances of a lack of a general regard for the general welfare. Whatever may be said in disproof of Calhoun's arguments for State rights, the accuracy of his remarks with regard to the position of rival sections has never been disputed. "The equilibrium between the two sections," he writes, "has been permanently destroyed. The Northern section in consequence will ever concentrate within itself the two majorities of which the government is composed; and should the Southern be excluded from all Territories now acquired, or to be hereafter acquired, it will soon have so decided a preponderance in the government and the Union as to be able to mould the Constitution to its pleasure. . . . . There can

with or without such a system for each of its parts."—Fisher's 'Trial of the Constitution,' p. 160.

be no safety for the weaker section. It places in the hands of the stronger and hostile section the power to crush her and her institutions, and leaves her no alternative but to resist, or sink down into a colonial condition."[7] Time has fully accomplished these predictions. The South is not only excluded from Territories, but her independent existence has been destroyed. There remain only ten or eleven millions of white citizens living under military surveillance in a great camp.

The indignation which Americans are accustomed to profess concerning the gloomy prophecies of European observers during the war of 1861–65, is a strange example of national forgetfulness and inconsistency. The separation of the States is the end which a large number of their greatest statesmen and publicists have constantly foretold. At least one half of the American people themselves either feared or believed that a dissolution of the Union was rendered inevitable by the revolt of the South. Fully as large a proportion of the public journals in America predicted that result as could be found in England, at any time during the war. It was not alone the Democratic press which uttered these prognostications. The organs of the Republican party were equally decided in their tone. The 'Tribune' is the most powerful organ of the Radicals, and on the 9th of November, 1860, it said,—"If the cotton States shall

7 'Disquisition on Government,' Calhoun's Works, i. p. 300.

become satisfied that they can do better out of the Union than in it, we insist on letting them go in peace." On the 26th of November following, Mr. Greeley again wrote as follows:—"If the cotton States unitedly and earnestly wish to withdraw peacefully from the Union, we think they should and would be allowed to do so. Any attempt to compel them by force to remain would be contrary to the principles enunciated in the immortal Declaration of Independence, contrary to the fundamental principles on which human liberty is based." Two other extracts from the writings of the same authority may be quoted:—"If it (the Declaration) justified the secession from the British empire of three millions of colonists in 1776, we do not see why it should not justify the secession of five millions of Southrons from the Union in 1861."[8] "Whenever it shall be clear that the great body of the Southern people have become exclusively alienated from the Union, and anxious to escape from it, we will do our best to forward their views."[9] Were the vaticinations and statements of English newspapers, so bitterly complained of, in any respect more unfavourable to the North than these? Every one engaged in American politics is aware that Mr. Lincoln and his cabinet, with but two exceptions, were convinced that the South must eventually triumph. It is not denied that at the present hour the Union is kept whole only by force—by the expedient,

[8] New York Tribune,' December 17th, 1860.

[9] Ibid. February 23rd, 1861.

often before recorded in history, of placing the conquered population under the absolute control of armies. These conditions are not, indeed, unalterable. The events which have been witnessed of late years may, under the best conceivable circumstances, leave no trace of angry feeling behind; the Southern people may be joined to the North again, and may forget the envenomed passions and animosities of the past; they may accept the new rule which has been prepared for them, and banish every feeling of resentment from their minds; they may excuse, or even justify, the treatment they have received since the war; all these things may happen in course of time, but no one can dispute that the first indication of so marvellous a change of public sentiment has yet to appear. What is palpable now, is that a party intensely hostile to the South rules at the North, and that it would be as easy to bring the poles together as these two sections of the Republic. There is no nearer approach to an era of universal peace, than is indicated by the establishment of an unmixed military despotism over almost as many States as were embraced within the original Constitution. This despotism may be necessary, but, though all the writers and all the public men of America endeavoured to prove that it was so, they could not but prove at the same time that while it exists there is no such thing as the Union, in the sense in which that title was given to the Confederated States by Washington and his contemporaries. That wholesome moderation on the part of the side gaining electoral victories which they constantly recommended is never practised. The contest is fierce, and passions are too much excited for the vanquished to be entitled to look for mercy when it is over. Such a struggle as that which the South challenged could not but excite a terrible spirit of vengeance. Yet the Northern people cannot suppose that it will be always safe to indulge this vengeance, or that they can keep the Southern people beneath their feet for ever. If their favourite argument with reference to Ireland be worth anything, it ought to do something more than supply them with a theme for impetuous denunciations of England. It ought to convince them of the danger of sowing the seeds of an internal hatred by misgovernment, and by the substitution of military for civil law. Every one is now prepared to admit that the negro has nothing further to gain by the abasement of his former owners. One of the black candidates for Congress has, indeed, declared that if elected he "will do his best to ameliorate the condition of the whites." Those who regard the Southern planters as scarcely fit objects for Christian charity, might find their worst wishes satisfied by this mockery of fate. But the ordinary, business-loving, peaceable citizen of the United States sees in this new Protectorate of the negro a source of endless future disaster. "Unless we read the signs of the times," remarks a recent writer, "and measure the antagonisms of race very incorrectly, the nation at large, should such an alternative be forced upon it, would sooner submit to a single dictator than to a million in the persons of black men."[10] There are, however, many who foresee that the negroes can no longer be excluded from political power, and therefore they reluctantly determine not to resist "progress" which they cannot prevent. Their judgment may not be fully justified by events, but it is at least possible that their anticipations will be partly accomplished, and that negroes will sit as legislators in the halls of the Capitol. To those who say that this is well, it is enough to reply that the American people have not yet decided to make negroes their rulers, and that a contest to settle that issue has still to be fought out.

In order to form even an imperfect judgment relative to the prospects of the duration of the political fabric in America, in its present form, it is necessary to understand the character of the people, and to appreciate properly that sentiment which I have frequently referred to as their "ideal." It is this ideal which reconciles the cultivated classes to many defects in the government which they would gladly remove, and which causes it to be essentially popular with the bulk of the people. They hope more from it than it has yet given, and no misfortunes that have happened shake the assurance that it will one day fully satisfy their expectations. They are proud of their country, because it has taken up a position of so much power and consequence in

[10] New York 'Round Table,' Oct. 5th, 1867.

the world at so early a period of its history, and they would eagerly make any sacrifice to preserve the Union which alone has made that position possible. But the future depends upon causes less under control than the exercise of will. The spirit in which the American people survey their responsibilities must greatly influence the destinies of the Union, and their aspirations and their character will not be without their effect. But there are other and mightier forces in action than these. It is impossible to bring fifty or a hundred millions of people together, scattered over a vast range of country, without having many conflicting interests immediately spring up. Wise beyond human conception, it might almost be said beyond human comprehension, would be the government which could exactly accommodate itself to all these interests, and exist for an extended period without giving any offence or doing any injustice. The advantages of the Union will always be partial, and the only plan of allaying discontent yet discovered is by keeping it down at the point of the bayonet. The intentions and aims of the American people are, doubtless, of a very noble and exalted character. Regarded in their highest form, they do not contemplate the future supremacy of their country over other nations, but they pursue a contest for principles which they believe to be essential to the happiness and welfare of mankind. Their imaginations are touched by those majestic visions of the coming days which their ablest public men have constantly conjured up before their eyes. They believe, with the devout faith with which men are accustomed to cling to their religion, that in America, as Emerson has told them,[11] is the seat and centre of the British race. There the individual always improves; the government exists only for his welfare, watching to ward off evil, but intermeddling with him no further. The strife of antagonistic classes is one day to be unknown, the sting of poverty will not be felt; there is plenty for all within easy reach, reckless prodigality or corruption can never entail burdens upon the people, or deprive them of the just fruits of their industry. As all men have an equal right to govern, so, if they are left to govern for themselves, they will be prosperous and contented. There are to be no wrongs inflicted by the powerful upon the defenceless; the voice of the oppressor is to be heard no more, the servant will be free from his master. "Under this system," in the words of an American writer, "the way is open for the realization of the most inspiring and most promising idea of modern Christian civilization,—the true brotherhood of man, in which man shall feel himself no longer an isolated individual, but shall find his completeness and perfection, his worth and his happiness, in the recognised relations of mutual dependence existing between himself and the community of which he forms an integral and essential part."[12]

---

11 'English Traits,' last chapter.

12 'North American Review,' Oct. 1865.

Such is the ideal. When the citizen of the United States speaks of the greatness and beauty of the American ideas, these are the ideas which he means; and he does not exaggerate their intrinsic charm, or the lustre which they reflect upon his national character. It is a great thing for a nation to possess ambition worthy of its place in the world; and that people might well be proud which contrived to solve all the undiscovered problems of government, and accomplished the objects hitherto restricted to republics of the imagination. But does the experience of eighty years of the American system justify these boasts or these anticipations? Do the people rest their claims to be considered the most enlightened nation of the world solely upon their material progress? Their wealth and strength, realised and potential, cannot disappoint their expectations. The constant tide of emigration keeps up the freshness and vigour of the race, and more than compensates for the wear and tear of life which the influences of climate, and the ever pressing desire to grow rich, inevitably entail.[13] But what of the moral and intellectual progress of the people? It has been great, no doubt, but is it commensurate with their advance in external marks of prosperity? Where is the candid and well-informed American who will prove that it is? The publications which issue from the press for the poorer classes are a

[13] Between 1820 and 1860 upwards of five millions of emigrants arrived in the country, of whom 2¾ millions were from the United Kingdom.—'Census Report of 1860.'

scandal to honest men. They are sold and read by thousands, and cannot be altogether without influence.[14] Nowhere are impostures of every kind, which are intended to deceive the ignorant, so common as in America. The execrable charlatans who prey upon the physical and mental fears of mankind are thicker than locusts in an Eastern field. They abound and prosper elsewhere, but it may safely be affirmed that in no part of the world are they so numerous and so rich, or ply their vocations with so much impunity and disregard of laws, as in the United States. Education does little or nothing for the common people in protecting them from the effects of the most ignorant delusions and the most abject superstitions. It would be an error to attach undue importance to such circumstances as these; but they demand mention, because they are among the things which prove that the national ideal is not yet attained. They show that the triumphs of knavery and folly, of ignorance and superstition, are renewed, and not ended, in the great Western world.

In the social life of the people, the influence of habits derived from imitations of another race is too plain to be overlooked, even by enthusiasts who acknowledge no imperfections in the government. It is

---

[14] See, for example, the 'Police Gazette,' the 'Police Intelligencer,' and the score of periodicals which cover the street-stalls and counters of common book-shops; or let a list be taken of the books which are vended in so public and well-known an establishment as Willard's Hotel, at Washington. Every respectable American passes them with loathing; but their sale is enormous.

essential to have a correct knowledge of this, in order to comprehend the almost invariable paradox of the American character. Some, indeed, attribute all these anomalies to the effect of climate alone. Even political differences have been traced to this cause. Thus, one writer tells us that "climate converted what had been merely different classes in England into distinct national types in America," and he repeats the idea in a thousand forms, and endeavours to give it cogency by many laborious illustrations.[15] The Americans are, as a rule, nervous, excitable, restless, impatient, quick-tempered, but withal kind-hearted, hospitable, and generous almost beyond description. A man might live many years among them without doing full justice to their disposition, but he would certainly end by becoming exceedingly attached to it. But there can be no motive for denying that French influences are plainly visible in the daily life of the nation, less so in New England than in other parts of the country, but everywhere in some degree. And even if New England were free from the infection, she is not America, but only a small portion of it, and we have no more right to take those five States as a model of the whole continent,

[15] Draper's 'History of the American Civil War,' New York, 1867. This writer appears to believe that a proper understanding of climatic influences would tend to prevent future political troubles. "Estrangement," he says, "subsides when men mutually begin to inquire into the philosophical causes of each other's obliquities; when they comprehend that there overrides so many of their apparently voluntary actions a necessary, an unavoidable constraint"—(p. 37).

than we have to take the city of New York. American writers often deplore the length to which their countrymen are inclined to carry their imitations of French manners and French ideas of domestic life. New England statisticians assert that of late years the aversion to a family has been growing more and more general.[16] The Americans are forming their national character under circumstances very different from those which their forefathers knew. The English have never, as Buckle points out, transplanted the manners and customs of France. French influence, he remarks, never affected the two most important classes in England, the "intellectual class and the industrial class." But there have been special circumstances to bring Americans into closer contact with the French than with the English. The services of Lafayette to the colonists are gratefully recalled, and, while England is remembered as an enemy, France is regarded as a hereditary friend. When Americans leave their business to obtain relaxation in travel, they naturally find more pleasure upon the boulevards of Paris than in the dingy streets of London. There is an element, too, in the disposition and temperament of the two nations which makes them agree. The Americans are fond of pleasure, and are happiest in the absence of conventionalities and the freedom from restraint.

There have also been political jealousies to keep

---

[16] See also a remarkable statement by Mr. Horace Greeley in a recent number of the 'New York Independent.' (July, 1867.)

the English and Americans asunder. Sometimes a dislike of England seems to be in the very fibre of the American character. There are Americans who are proud of their descent, or who owe their education to the mother country, and would not give up their part in the glories of her history and her literature for all the small national differences which were ever fostered by the perversity or the vanity of man. But there are some with whom jealousy of England amounts to a disease of the intellectual faculties, and who angrily resent from an Englishman the faintest echo of criticism which their own press or public men pronounce unchallenged. National antipathies and passions cannot always be explained or accounted for, and they are sometimes the most dangerous when their sources are unknown. The most recent complaint of Americans is, that they were traduced and misrepresented by English writers during their war—but have they nothing to complain of on this score from other countries? French writers were not less hostile to them and their cause; but they do not hate France. In her case they prefer to obey the Scriptural injunction, and love those who despitefully use them. So, too, as it has been shown, their own press was charged with heavier accusations against the national character, and drew a darker representation of the part which the North played in the war, and more systematically misrepresented the deeds of the Northern armies, than the newspapers of all the rest of the world put together. Would the Americans, the greatest lovers of liberty alive, deny to English publicists the same freedom of speech and opinion which their own countrymen enjoy?

But, in truth, America has always averted her face from England, as England too often has averted hers from America. In such an unfortunate estrangement as this, it would answer no good purpose to inquire which has given the greatest cause of offence. But it may fairly be said that in England there is not found a class of politicians who make it one object of their lives to stir up the prejudices of their countrymen against America, to poison their minds with misstatements and false representations, and to endeavour to raise a popular demand for war. There is a class of politicians in America who find it profitable to act thus in relation to England. But we are not to blame the native-born American. He may sometimes join in the cry to win an election, but his better sense and judgment recoil from the work. The anti-English feeling in America is part of the legacy of Irish hatred which we have inherited from those who have gone before us. Thousands of emigrants who leave the British Isles for the New World quit them with a curse in their hearts. The sense of injury inspires them with undying hatred. The Irishman has never heard his poverty and his hardships ascribed to any other cause but the oppression of England, and he hates fiercely the enemy who has inflicted all these wrongs upon his race. The English or Scotch labourer who emigrates to America does so, not in discontent or anger, but in order to provide for himself and his family better means of support than are at his command, as he believes, in his own land. So far from hating his country, it is sometimes many years before he conquers that home sickness which is the worst burden of the dweller in strange lands. To emigrants such as these, there is no present so acceptable as an English book or an English newspaper. They follow the political events of their mother country with as keen an interest as if they had never left it. As time passes on, and they grow prosperous, their desire to return may grow stronger, but they are less fit than ever to go back to renew a life of toil, and moreover there is a family to provide for. Thus they settle down, and their children grow up to be proud of the English name and their inherited share in the illustrious renown which she has won. This is the story of many an American home. But with the Irish emigrant all is different. He lands with a grievance exuding from every pore. Upon this class the unscrupulous or the ignorant politician works at his pleasure. The Irishman is easily fusible, and the party leader understands how to manage him. A pretext for abusing or threatening England is never lacking. It is impossible to please a person who is determined to be dissatisfied, and the task is not easier when it is attempted with a nation. President Jackson, in his message to Congress in 1829, referred to America and England in these terms:—"Everything in the condition and history of the two nations is calculated to inspire sentiments of mutual respect, and to carry conviction to the minds of both that it is their policy to preserve the most cordial relations." Such language as this has been rare in the messages of Presidents, or the despatches of American Foreign Secretaries, in later years. The good sense, the forbearance, and the patience of both peoples, may yet root up animosities which are as mischievous as they are unfounded. There is no good to be done in the world comparable to that of bringing America and England into bonds of cordial friendship. The work which England has tried to do, not without many heavy sacrifices, nor without many successes, of maintaining freedom and spreading enlightenment in the world, must one day be taken up by America. England, whatever faults may be ascribed to her by the hirelings of Trades' Unions, or the creatures of a faction, has struck many a blow for freedom when there was none other to strike it, and she has ere now accomplished such work as no true child or descendant of hers will ever seek to dishonour. If there be any truth in the theory of the necessary decadence of nations, the day must come when her power will depart from her, and when even her glory must rest upon tradition. In that day America will be covered with hundreds of millions of free men, and upon them must fall the responsibilities and duties which the small island in the midst of the sea, long wielding an influence altogether disproportionate to its physical means, endeavoured in ancient times to discharge. If America could hasten the decay of England by a few years, what would she have gained by destroying a power which showed her how to be free by keeping the sacred fire of freedom alive through generations when it was extinguished and all was dark elsewhere, and which with her presents to this day the only formidable barrier against the dominion of a hostile race? England and America are the natural allies of the world, and they are kept apart by brawls which would disgrace a community of quarrelsome villagers.

With France, happily for the peace of mankind, it is not so. Occasional misunderstandings between France and America have arisen, but the Americans are persistent in their resolve not to take offence at anything which Frenchmen say or Frenchmen write. This indifference to criticism in one direction, and an excessive sensitiveness to it in another, might be regarded as an involuntary testimony to the high estimation in which Americans hold the English judgment; but such conclusions are an unworthy mockery of the question. Since France is preferred, can we wonder that French manners influence social life in the United States more than English manners? Formerly, travellers concurred in bearing witness to the simplicity of the habits of Americans. Some of De Tocqueville's remarks on this subject seem now as if they were written in a tone of cynicism which he rarely betrayed. The morality of the people he describes as being so supernaturally pure that he is obliged to travel beyond the ordinary range of human motives to account for it. He traces it to the equality of conditions of all classes. In aristocratic communities, people who have a fondness for each other cannot always marry, and "nature secretly avenges herself for the constraint imposed upon her by the laws of man."[17] But in America, where a woman knows that there are no social prejudices to forbid her marriage with any man she may happen to love, she never does wrong, and married life is unsullied, because all marriages are made from motives of affection. Besides this security of national virtue, we are assured that the busy life which Americans lead "distracts them from the passion of love, by *denying them time to indulge it.*"[18] This is one of the passages of M. de Tocqueville's work which has never failed to amuse the American reader. And again he says — "In America all books, novels not excepted, suppose women to be chaste, and no one thinks of relating affairs of gallantry."[19]

---

17 'Democracy in America,' chap. xi. vol. ii. p. 250. (Tome iii. p. 332.)

18 Ibid. p. 254. (Tome iii. p. 337.)

19 Ibid. p. 250. (Tome iii. p 331.)

No one supposes that the Americans are less moral or religious as a people than other nations, but De Tocqueville's observations seem to be slander disguised as irony and caricature. In the midst of his romantic picture, he occasionally introduces some true touches. He was obliged to own that he found a taste for self-indulgence among the people, and various circumstances have occurred since his time to give an impetus to the race for wealth and the love of display. "The love of well-being," he remarks,[20] "is now become the predominant taste of the nation; the great current of human passions runs in that channel, and sweeps everything along its course." But it was necessary that he should reconcile this opinion with the opposite statement that he had made. He could only do it by assigning miraculous virtues to Democracy. He says, in a passage which almost reads like a burlesque of his opinions by a malicious critic, "The passion for physical gratifications produces in Democracies effects very different from those which it occasions in aristocratic nations."[21] He might as well have asserted that the passion for stealing one's neighbour's goods, or coveting one's neighbour's wife, is a vice in monarchies and a virtue in Democracies. Fortunately for the purposes of sober judgment, M. de Tocqueville supplies us with illustrations of his meaning:—"To build enormous palaces,

---

[20] 'Democracy in America,' chap. x. vol. ii. p. 157. (Tome iii. p. 211.) [21] Ibid. chap. xi. vol. ii. p. 158. (Tome, iii. p. 212.)

to conquer or to mimic nature, to ransack the world in order to gratify the passions of a man, *is not thought of*." Even when De Tocqueville visited the country such a remark as this could only have been founded on the most partial observation, like another of his statements, that "in the North the majority of servants are either freedmen or the children of freedmen"[22]—which, as his American editor justly points out, is the mistake of a stranger who judges of a country from its hotels. The experience of any one who has seen an American city or its suburbs—the Wabash or Michigan Avenues of Chicago, the environs of St. Louis or Cincinnati, the Brookline of Boston, the Fifth Avenue of New York, the palatial residences of Newport or Long Branch—must give a different impression of the habits of the American people from that which M. de Tocqueville conveys. An American writer, speaking of his own country, says,—"As a people we are lavish beyond any other in our personal habits and ways of living. The extravagance of the rich in dress, equipages, and entertainments is noticeable at home, and too often generates abroad into an ostentation more conspicuous than creditable."[23] Nor is M. de Tocqueville less in error when he says "that the inhabitants of North America look upon literature properly so called with a kind of

[22] 'Democracy in America,' chap. v.
[23] 'New York Times,' Sept. 26, 1867.

disapprobation,"[24] or that, "in the civil service, none of the American functionaries *can be said to be removable;* the places which some of them occupy are inalienable, and the others are chosen for a term which cannot be shortened."[25] The latter statement was never at any time supported by facts. The very opposite is true—*all* officers being easily removable, except the judges of the Federal Supreme Court.

If the character of the nation were to be drawn by an American with a perfectly impartial hand, it would be found neither so exalted as its professed panegyrists depict it, nor so full of faults as adverse critics have sometimes led us to suppose. That the Americans have peculiarities of temperament and disposition they will admit, nor are these peculiarities anything to their discredit. Nervousness, excitability, and restlessness are characteristics which may probably be traced in some degree to the lax discipline which prevails in the training of the young. The theory of Dr. Draper upon climatic influences, is at least valuable as another proof that the existence of extreme differences among the people of various sections of the Union, is recognised by all classes of American writers.

De Tocqueville, however, gave the weight of his authority to the statement that there were no hostile interests to be found in the Union. The result of

---

[24] 'Democracy in America,' vol. i. p. 403. (Tome ii. p. 233.)
[25] Ibid. ib. p. 136. (Tome i. pp. 180-181.)

his travels and reflections was to convince him that it was "almost impossible to discover any private interest which might now tempt a portion of the Union to separate from the other States."[26] "It is easy indeed," he says again, "to discover different interests in the different parts of the Union, but I am unacquainted with any which are hostile to each other."[27] American writers of the highest authority might have led him to other conclusions. So, too, he affirms that no natural barriers divide the people, forgetting that, when the Pacific slope became peopled, the Rocky Mountains would lie between their inhabitants and the Atlantic States. "The inhabitants of the South," he remarks elsewhere, "are induced to support the Union in order to avail themselves of its protection against the blacks"—a curious misapprehension of the relationship which existed at that time between the two races, and an instance of the failure of his foresight not less remarkable than his well-known prediction, that, if any States ever desired to leave the Union, no attempt would be made to restrain them, or would fail if made."[28]

Some other statements of this distinguished writer serve to present in a clear light the change which of late years has passed over the government in all its relations. "The Union," he remarks, "is a vast body, which presents no definite object to patriotic

[26] 'Democracy in America,' vol. ii. p. 250.
[27] Ibid. vol. i. p. 503. (Tome ii. p. 358.)
[28] Ibid. vol. i. pp. 497-99 and 500. (Tome ii. p. 343 *et seq.*)

feeling. . . . The tendency of the interests, the habits, and the feelings of the people is to centre political activity in the States in preference to the Union."[29] And again he says, "The Federal government is, therefore, notwithstanding the precautions of those who founded it, naturally so weak, that, more than any other, it requires the free consent of the governed to enable it to subsist."[30] These, and many other observations of the same nature, show that M. de Tocqueville had failed to penetrate the real sentiment of the American people. Any man of intelligence with whom he conversed in the South would have expressed to him the views which are summed up in the foregoing passages, and his chapter on the prospects of the duration of the Union might almost have been written by John C. Calhoun. It is a faithful reflex of Southern feeling. But it gave a false impression of the *national* feeling. The attachment to the Federation, on account of the dignity and power which it gave to all its members, was always latent in a majority of the people, and when they were called upon to choose between that and the indulgence of local passions, they would certainly throw everything aside for the sake of clinging fast to the common bond. The Federation was entered into in despite of internal derangements, and, if its value as a source of strength was perceived in 1789, it was not probable that it would be depreciated in 1861. The

[29] 'Democracy in America,' vol. i. p. 496. (Tome ii. p. 350.)

[30] Ibid p. 497. (Tome ii. p. 351.)

great point that remained to be tested was whether the integrity of States was consistent with the continual development of the central power. Slavery led to the issue being tried and decided long before it might otherwise have arisen, but it could not always have been hidden or evaded. There has now occurred a general dislocation of the government. The Federal principle rises supreme; the State principle is weakened. We see the people of the United States embarking in what is essentially a new plan of government, in which their past experience will be of little service to them. Slavery is gone, but the pitiless enmities excited by slavery have been touched with fresh fire. It was not the four millions of men and women in bondage which constituted the great danger of the Union. It was the passionate dispute over them, which knew no cessation, that broke up the peace of the country. The position of the negro has been reversed: from the slave he has become the ruler; the destinies of his former masters have been committed to his hands; but he is still the object of the bitterest dissensions which ever agitated a people. The settlement of the radical disagreement between the North and the South has not been attempted. A desire for revenge has been added to the other resentful impulses of the Southern section, and the negro, whom the North released from slavery, but will not make politically free, is still the formidable agent of disunion. If the North had been perfectly just in its measures on behalf of what it calls "human freedom," the exasperation of the South might not have been so terrible. It boasted of its intentions to give the negro the rights of a citizen, while it systematically denied them to him in its own division of the country. Why did Connecticut, Pennsylvania, and Ohio, within the space of a few months past, refuse to sanction negro suffrage by overwhelming majorities? They helped to force negro suffrage upon the South. They were among the foremost to demand the full and complete enfranchisement of the liberated slave. They did not, it is true, ever attempt to assert that they went to war with the South for the abolition of slavery. That may have been the theory of a few extremists, but the bulk of the people never thought of slavery —they went to war to save the Union, and to preserve the honour of their flag. The extremists could afterwards enter the field, covered with the dead bodies of those whom they hated, and shout what cries of exultation they pleased, for the masses who fought had retired, and the foe was silent. If the desire to do justice to the negro was so universal in the North as the English people have often been assured, why do not the Northern States invest him now with political rights? Why does Ohio turn away from her counsels in disgrace the men who came to her with negro suffrage in their hands? Because the Northern people at heart are weary of the negro, and his wrongs, and his pretensions, and his champions, and all that appertains to him. They turn him loose in the South that he may be a scourge to the people who strove to destroy the government —they give him licence, not because they love him, but because they wish to avenge themselves upon his masters, and to hold up a fearful warning to all advocates of secession who may come hereafter.

Whether the Union will exist or perish is beyond the power of human discernment to determine, but it may safely be affirmed that it will never be dissolved without a struggle as fierce as that which closed in 1865. Is it to be supposed that, while all the rest of the world perceive plainly that division would be a fatal blow to American power, the American people are blind to the fact? They are ambitious; they have unbounded faith and belief in themselves. In all probability, even had the South gained its independence, so strong is the influence of a patriotic feeling, that it would always have readily united with the North against the attacks of any third power. Americans are anxious to grow in power as a nation, and they know that the Union offers them the means of gratifying this desire. Warned by the disastrous experience of the Southern people, what other section of the community will ever be willing to fight as they have fought, only to suffer as they have suffered? That bloody and unequal struggle will not be renewed, or, if it be, the abettors of it may see their fate reflected in that vast and unhappy region which extends from the Potomac to the Rio Grande, and which is covered this day with mourning women and desolate homes.

Yet great popular commotions may occur. That element of the government which has always seemed to be the best security for its stability, namely, the integrity of the States, has been much shattered in the convulsions of recent years. "The great mass of legislation," said President Jackson in his first annual message, "relating to our internal affairs, was intended to be left where the Federal Convention found it—in the State governments. Nothing is clearer, in my view, than that we are chiefly indebted for the success of the Constitution under which we are now acting to the watchful and auxiliary operation of the State authorities." Once establish a precedent, no matter on what pretext, for breaking down the State systems by the Federal arm, and the future is chaos. Who shall say what party, what majority, may rule next? In our own time we see States deprived of their "equal rights," denied the right of representation, compelled to accept laws made for them by the Federal Congress in which they are not allowed to have a voice, the press liable to *avertissements*, the pulpit coerced or suborned, and the ballot-box handed over almost exclusively to a race which, in reasoning powers, is not far superior to the creatures of the field. Every one of these measures may be indispensable in the eyes of the majority, but is any one of them consistent with the former principles of the Union, or with a faultless incorporation of liberty and freedom which some Americans believe they were the first to discover, and will be the last to defend? Had the doctrine that each State shall be permitted to reserve the right to manage its internal affairs been transmitted to posterity, the Union, with the curse of slavery removed from it, might have defied the hand of time. But now the individual parts are subjected to a power resembling the centrifugal force of the physical world. Leave each State free to order its own concerns, and it would have signified little by what name the general government was called, or how wide was the area over which it extended. There would have been the strength of a nation, with untrammelled local governments. But State institutions have been formally placed at the mercy of the majority. To-day it is the Republicans who are wielding the lash; in a short time they in their turn may be brought under its stroke. To-day they and they only decide what the Constitution means; to-morrow their antagonists may claim the heaven-sent gift of reading it aright.

"Upon this country," said Jackson to his countrymen in the message just quoted, "more than any other, has, in the providence of God, been cast the special guardianship of the great principle of adherence to written Constitutions. If it fail here, all hope in regard to it will be extinguished." The words of this solemn warning are as lifeless as he who uttered them. The "sacred law" is only brought out, like the great car of the Hindoos, to be decked with the popular deities, and driven over the necks of the minority. It wears the colours of every side which happens to govern. Where are the unalterable principles of which "the fathers" boasted? Once tamper with the fundamental law of the land, the law by which alone the separate fragments could cohere, and all other changes are easy. There was once a power in the Union which said, "This shall be done and the other shall not be done." But it is destroyed—mainly, in the first instance, by the arrogance and folly of the minority, but not the less effectually destroyed. One step after another has been taken, until at last the "sacred law" is scoffed at, and those who expounded it seem like the teachers of an exploded school of philosophy. "No man," remarked President Van Buren, writing of Hamilton, "better understood than he that the inviolate sanctity of a written Constitution was the life of a republican government, and that its days were numbered from the moment its people and rulers ceased thus to preserve, protect, and defend it."[31] But where are now the safeguards upon which all eminent Americans who have ever lived chiefly depended for the permanence of the Union—the integrity of State rights, and

[31] 'Political Parties, p. 213.

the universal obedience to the Constitution? The storms of ninety years undermined them, and the shock of a civil war completed their ruin. It would have been little had the Constitution been altered in accordance with the prescribed forms, for then all the people would have been parties to it, and the new law would have had indisputable sanction. But it has been seized by one side as an instrument of party warfare, and the other side is denied the privileges which it guaranteed to all. Unless this course be changed, the government will pass wholly into the hands of unscrupulous partisans, and even the moral influence of men of independent character will be lost. The great scholars of the country will be disposed to abandon the very discussion of politics in despair. At this time we find that they have some hope. Already some of the foremost men are earnestly calling attention to the progress the nation is making towards a rule of anarchists. Mr. Curtis, the historian of the Constitution, thus appeals to his countrymen in a contemporary journal:[32]—"A great change has come over us. From being a people whose regard for law was proverbial, and whose standard of right and wrong in political action invariably and instinctively referred itself to the positive texts of a written Constitution, we have come to witness with indifference, and to accept as

[32] The 'New York World.'

matters o. course, methods of public action which can be justified by no existing constitutional principles, which are at variance with the conceded nature of our institutions, which violate solemn public charters, and which rest upon nothing but the temporary popular judgment of what is expedient, or, more frequently, upon a passionate popular determination to effect certain objects by direct force. No thoughtful person can well deny that such is our present condition. The most unanswerable appeals to the plainest constitutional provisions, made as impressively as undeniable truth can make them, and made from quarters which at any former period of our history would have commanded instant and general attention, are now received by a large part of the people of this country with apathy. We pay very little heed to anything but the object that is to be accomplished. Whether that object be lawful—whether, if it is lawful, the methods by which we propose to reach it are permitted by the law—we have almost wholly ceased to consider. Respect for the law, because it is the law; loyal obedience to its commands, because they are its commands; chivalrous submission to restraint, because a lawful authority has created a restraint, are not now among our prominent national characteristics. At this moment, it cannot be said that a majority of the people of this country are faithful to the obligations of fundamental law; and it is more than probable that one of the chief reasons for this is, a general ignorance of the sources and of the morally binding character of those obligations."

In an equally impressive manner one of the principal Republican Senators, Mr. Trumbull, who has taken a leading part in all measures for the enfranchisement and protection of the negroes, has lately warned the people that their government cannot last without a fixed permanent law. "The fundamental law," he says, "known as the Constitution, emanating directly from the sovereign people, and placing on their representatives limitations in the exercise of power, can never be disregarded without endangering private rights and the public liberties of the people, as well as the existence of the Union of which it forms the truest security. . . . To trust representatives with unlimited discretion, or allow them to exercise powers not granted, would be to make them the masters instead of the servants of the people, and such a representative government would be little better than despotism." These appeals to the sober sense of the community may not be heeded, and all the dangers which are predicted may be brought about, but the last chance remains that when the present angry strife is over, the people will return to their full allegiance to laws which are their truest protection, and their security for coming times.

This review of the changes of eighty years, and the prospects now before the Union, cannot be closed without a reference to one other subject. The existence of a large national debt is sometimes regarded as one of the perils of the Union, but, if wisely managed, it might prove an element of strength. It is essentially the debt of the people. They not only approved the war, but made it, and invited the Federal government, as well as the governments of their States, to raise any amount of revenue they required by means of taxation. To pay this debt is a point of honour with the Americans, and it is impossible to believe that they will ever seek to repudiate the obligation. But the gross mismanagement of the debt, and the heavy pressure of taxation, may encourage a certain section of politicians to evade that obligation. Thus, an argument has been addressed to the people by ex-General Butler, to the effect that the interest on that important part of the national securities, known as the five-twenties, ought to be paid in currency and not in gold. Technically, Mr. Butler may be right. The five-twenty bonds, of subsequent issues, to August 1861, did not expressly promise to pay the interest in "coin." But there cannot be a doubt that the people subscribed for them on the faith that both principal and interest would be paid in coin, and this view is supported by the Secretary of the Treasury. His decision may help to re-inspire public confidence in the debt, but the fact that it is constantly open to the suggestion of repudiation, in one form or other, is a great misfortune to the people. They are obliged to pay a much higher rate of interest than would otherwise be required of them in the market, and their natural credit is constantly questioned, while they are making vast sacrifices to support it. And, plainly, this is one effect of popular government. Hundreds of thousands of voters in the United States do not hold bonds. and know nothing more about the debt than that they are taxed on account of it. Their votes are as valuable as the votes of any other class. If they are to be caught by whispers of repudiation, these whispers will not be wanting. There is no voter without his mouthpiece. No doubt the bulk of the people are animated by sincere intentions with regard to their debt, and their anger at the merest suggestion from abroad that they will not pay it, may be accepted as a sign of their good faith. But they cannot stop the mouths of demagogues. They suffer, because there is a class among them, equal with themselves at the polls, who care much for their immediate personal interests, and little for the interests of their country, and who are not at all eager to pay the debt. Thus, the bonds are low, and the United States seem never likely to be relieved from the burden of interest at six per cent. The hopes of some are supported by the fallacious promises of early liquidation. Various expedients for this process have been laid before the public. The Secretary of the Treasury, in his report for 1864-5, proposed to raise two hundred millions a year, by taxation, over and above the sums required for the current expenses of the government. This, he said, would extinguish the debt in from twenty-eight to thirty-two years, according to the rate of interest. But his scheme passes all the ordinary bounds even of American patience. Can it be for a moment supposed that the country would endure the additional taxation which the Secretary suggests? The excitement of war led the people to pay taxes almost without noticing the amount, but now they are sitting down with cooled blood to weigh the cost. They could not support these fresh demands, even if they were willing to comply with them. As one of their writers remarks, Mr. M'Culloch's plan "ignores all natural laws of commerce, and, while it proposes to draw heavily and continually on the resources of the country, it does not consider how those resources will be affected by the process. It would not only," he contends, "put an end to the debt but to commerce also."

It is little less than a marvel that commerce flourishes at all in the United States. It is hampered by a thousand artificial appliances for checking its growth. The system of taxation is now perceived to be not only extravagant and oppressive, but ruinous to trade, in consequence of the repetition of the taxes in successive processes of production, and similar blunders. The special commissioner appointed by the United States Government to inquire into the taxation and revenue, stated that "if the ratio of taxation in Great Britain had been in 1865 the same as that now maintained in the United States, the amount derived from taxation in that country would have been 1,424,184,840 dollars in place of 354,131,000."[33]

The debt is managed without any regard to the interests of the people, or even to the ultimate profit of the exchequer. It is so confused and intricate that no one professes thoroughly to understand it. It offers six different rates of interest, and its bonds have nineteen different periods of maturity. There are no less than twelve different kinds of bonds carrying six per cent., issued under the authority of as many Acts of Congress. "Our public debt," says a recent writer, "is in such a state of confusion as to be entirely out of reach of the popular understanding, and correspondingly out of the popular confidence. Every contingency is turned into a trick of speculation. Rates, maturities, and liabili-

---

33 'Report of Mr. David A. Wells,' p. 43. The following statistical facts are given by this gentleman :—

"The revenue derived from taxation in the United States in 1866 was 561,572,266 dollars; and the value of real and personal property, according to the census of 1860, 14,282,726,088 dollars. The amount of revenue derived in Great Britain from various forms of taxation in 1864-65, excluding the receipts from crown lands, post-office, &c., was 354,131,000 dollars; the value of real and personal property, according to the census of 1861, being 31,512,000,000 dollars, the estimated increase of three per cent. per annum, or fifteen per cent., advancing the value in 1866 to 36,238,800,000 dollars.

ties, are mixed together at every point, and it is not in the ability, if it were the interest, of dealers to explain them."[34] In addition to the Federal debt of over two thousand six hundred millions, there are the State debts, which make the burden on the American citizen very little less in amount than that which is borne by the British subject, while the mode of levying taxes is immensely more vexatious in America than in England.[35]

The commercial policy of the nation is equally unfavourable to the interests of the people. It is calculated that the American labourer pays from twenty-five to thirty-three per cent of his average earnings in direct taxation.[36] The policy of protection and prohibitory tariffs, which the Republican party has made its own, is the only really serious clog which exists to the national progress. New England, the stronghold of protection, has suffered in some parts from its effects.[37] The manufactures which have flourished

---

[34] See a little work on 'The Public Debt of the United States,' by J. S. Gibbons (New York, 1867), p. 39.

[35] The 'New Englander,' for August, 1867, estimates that the American citizen's share of the entire public debt is "within 3 59 dollars of the *per capita* of the more favoured British subject." The 'Evening Post,' of July 19th, 1867, complains that in the United States about sixteen thousand articles are taxed. Mr. Cox, an ex-member of Congress, recently told the people of Ohio that in America the working man is taxed higher per head than in any other country in the world.

[36] 'Evening Post,' 24th July, 1867.

[37] See a pamphlet on 'The Collection of the Revenue,' by Edward Atkinson (Boston, 1867), p. 37.

most in the United States—such as machinery, agricultural implements, and tools—are those which have never been protected at all.[38] Production has been limited to an extent which alarms some of the Republicans themselves.[39] The foreign trade of the country has declined with incredible rapidity. In 1853 the amount of American tonnage engaged in foreign trade was about fifteen per cent. in excess of that of Great Britain; at the beginning of 1867 it was more than thirty-three per cent. less. The decrease was thus nearly fifty per cent. The decline in the coastwise and inland trade has been about twelve per cent. Shipbuilding has been almost wholly transferred to the British Provinces. "Our finances," remarks a competent writer in an American journal, "have been managed in ignorance or in defiance of fundamental law. There is a universal torpor creeping over the industrial energies of the

---

[38] See a pamphlet on 'The Collection of the Revenue,' by Edward Atkinson (Boston, 1867), p. 37.

[39] "Mr. Atkinson obtained some statistics from Deputy-Commissioner Harland touching the number of persons in the United States paying income-tax, or, in other words, having an income of over six hundred dollars a year, in 1866; from which it appears that not over half a million out of a population of thirty-six millions have more than enough to support a family in the plainest way; of course, of these a large number must find it difficult to make ends meet at all. As long as America, although the richest country in the world, and that which presents fewest inequalities of fortune, has this story to tell, it can hardly be said that it does not need to produce more rapidly, or in greater abundance."—'North American Review,' July, 1867, pp. 210, 211.

nation. Manufactures are being rooted out, every department of trade and industry is languishing, the public revenues are being destroyed, and a huge debt accumulating abroad." So dear are all the necessities of life that the labouring man who emigrates to the United States scarcely ever improves his position, unless he has been unable to find regular employment in his own land.[40] When the Federal government required only 60,000,000 of dollars a year, and obtained it chiefly by customs and land sales, the deductions from the earnings of the working man were inconsiderable. But now the central government raises over 500,000,000 by customs and internal revenue alone, and taxation, as we have seen, is very little lower than it is in England, while every article required for the household or the person is immensely dearer.

It would be idle to suppose that these circumstances will not have any effect upon the future of the country; possibly they may be henceforth a fruitful source of bickering and strife between the various States whose interests are most injuriously affected. But the national debt was contracted for an object of which all approved, and all will aid in honourably discharging it. The poorest native-born American in the country would not willingly attach

[40] "The industrial classes have been growing worse off, able to purchase less, and to save less; this poverty re-acts on both traders and manufacturers."—'American Annual Cyclopædia,' 1866.

to the national name the everlasting stigma of repudiating liabilities which were incurred for the preservation of the Republic. If the day should arrive when their legislation is conducted by men of character and principle, their eyes will be opened to many of their present mistakes and delusions on questions of political economy. At present the people are saved from serious commercial troubles chiefly by their boundless confidence in themselves, and by their elastic temperament. They recover so soon from a blow that they never seem to feel it. Their business men marvel at the recurrent "panics" which are so common in England, and are accustomed to say that the English merchants are losing their ancient courage. A banker once remarked to me, "If any people in the world are fairly entitled to a financial panic once a week, we certainly are that people. But we do not have it, because we *know* that we shall pull through." While they have this faith, they will be able to conquer their difficulties, or at least to meet them with spirit.

There are no dangers from without to threaten the Union, but it may be justly questioned whether the present generation have been so careful as their forefathers tried to be of the securities within. The era of general agreement, and deep-seated satisfaction with the government, is more remote than it was in the days when the founders of the Constitution committed it with affectionate solicitude to the care of their posterity. It has been shown in the foregoing pages, and the proofs might have been multiplied indefinitely, that a great minority of the people chafe and fret under the yoke of a government which, in theory, affords perfect freedom and satisfaction to all. It is still common to find Americans writing of their country in terms like these:—"The career of the Republic has thus far consisted of two steps. It first became, in practice, a pure democracy, and then an oligarchy of demagogues; the worst of all possible forms of misgovernment."[41] But, in addition to this kind of dissatisfaction, there are numberless Americans who have no sympathy with the wishes or designs of that class of their countrymen who maintain that the democratic theory can never be carried too far. They are far from believing that an unchecked democracy is the best and soundest form of government. They would place some limit upon the exercise of the franchise; and they insist upon the inexpediency of allowing incapable and inexperienced persons to vote. But what present hope is there for men who hold these opinions? The course of national "levelling" is swift and irresistible, and what is once yielded to clamour can never be withdrawn. Only in countries where a rule of Democracy has never been tried is it praised and coveted. The American is as much attached to class

41 'Southern Review,' vol. i. p. 350. (Baltimore, 1867).

distinctions as the citizen of any other country. He does not consort by preference with those beneath him in station. He does not ask the ignorant to sit by his fireside, and he would not allow them to neutralise his influence in political life if he could avoid it. But he knows that one of the results of eighty years' trial of republican institutions is the transfer of power from men of the character of Washington to men of the character of Butler and Thaddeus Stevens; and this has been effected by the agency of the needy and illiterate orders. The great men of his country who have passed away were not those who filled the highest post in the government. Daniel Webster and Henry Clay were men too greatly gifted to be taken up by party intriguists, and supported by the numerous classes. The Americans do not pride themselves upon a democratic government, except when they are sometimes writing or speaking for foreign readers. They wished to keep many things which they have lost, but the tide of popular will quietly defied their control. We find American writers dwelling upon the "dangers of democracy" with an earnestness which ought to convince theorists elsewhere that there is, after all, some danger in intrusting the larger share of political power to the least educated classes. In America the truth has long been admitted that Democracy is insatiable. Its demands increase in volume and vehemence with every attempt to set them at rest.

In such a system, everything worth keeping by a community is dependent solely upon the self-restraint of that class which is under the least temptation to practice self-restraint. In times of tumult and agitation, the sober and correcting influence of experience and education is likely to be of benefit; but there are no means of bringing this influence into operation, unless the people themselves desire it. How often will they be willing to call in outer aid to restrain themselves? The moving forces of any community which once makes an approach to democracy must ever impel it towards great organic change. The nature of man is to be dissatisfied with that which he has. Whatever may be his condition, his instincts suggest to him that in some other condition he would be better off. Individuals seek for change, and nations thirst for it with a restless longing. When they are made aware that they can alter any part of their government at pleasure, permanence of construction is out of the question. As time passes on, the people of America will be brought to the knowledge of the truth, that a finished system of government is only to be arrived at, if mankind is ever destined to enjoy the blessing at all, after many failures, and by the exercise of forbearance and wisdom on a more general scale than has hitherto been common in the world. Every system promises perfection until it is put into action, and it is only in rare cases that those who watch its working agree tc shut their eyes to its inadequateness. In America a habit so fatal to the hope of improvement is fast disappearing. Americans care less for foreign criticism than ever they did, because they respect themselves more, and because they know their own strength. Their history is but now beginning, and their national character exhibits many unexpected modifications. Their former misjudged admiration for everything American, in political theory, has been transferred to a school of politicians in Europe, who have special purposes to serve in producing social disturbances, and who blindly praise what they have never seen, and ignorantly admire what they do not understand. By political men of a nobler type, no object ought to be sought after more earnestly than that of making the working men of these islands familiar with every detail of the American Government as it actually exists. The whole truth ought to be laid before them, stripped of the disguises of the doctrinaire, or the narrow and bigoted conceit of the spurious philosopher. Let the English working men see and understand the American Government as the men who are engaged in its administration see it, and they will soon be jealous of changes in their own. They will learn to prize a civil system which is essentially what the intelligence and spirit of the whole people, and not of any class, have made it, which has awakened from time to time the admiration of the world, and which is at this hour more just and fair in its method of working than any other polity known to mankind. The future of England may not be so full of freshness and promise as that of America, but we have won an immortal past, and we still have much in our laws which Americans desire, and hitherto have desired in vain. That they may succeed in building up a government which will secure to them for all time to come the enjoyment of constitutional freedom, must be the hope of us all; and their efforts to consummate this glorious work ought not to be retarded by the undiscriminating adulation of men who invent wrongs for others in order that they may obtain influence of which they are unworthy, and use it afterwards to the disadvantage of an ancient Kingdom which has been assailed by many demagogues, and hitherto survived them all.

THE END.

LONDON: PRINTED BY WILLIAM CLOWES AND SONS, STAMFORD STREET, AND CHARING CROSS.

CHARLES SCRIBNER. A. C. ARMSTRONG. A. J. PEABODY.

Condensed Catalogue

OF THE PUBLICATIONS OF

CHARLES SCRIBNER & Co.,

654 BROADWAY,

NEW YORK.

⁂ *The figures in the last column of this Catalogue refer to* CHARLES SCRIBNER & CO.'S *Descriptive Catalogue, copies of which will be sent to any address upon application.*

⁂ *Blanks in the column of prices, except in the case of School Text-Books, the prices of which may be learned from* CHARLES SCRIBNER & CO.'S *Educational Catalogue, indicate that the Works are either out of print or in press.*

⁂ *In this list the names of Books just published are given in* SMALL CAPITALS ; *those issued during the year* 1867, *as well as new editions of Works previously produced, are indicated by italics.*

⁂ *The prices here given are for the regular style of binding in cloth. Books furnished in other styles, and their respective prices, may be learned from the Descriptive Catalogue.*

⁂ *Any of these Books will be sent post-paid to any address upon receipt of the price.*

	Volumes.	Size.	Price.	Page
ADAMS, W., D.D.				
THANKSGIVING	1	12mo	$2 00	2
Three Gardens	1	12mo	2 00	1
AGASSIZ, PROF. LOUIS.				
Structure of Animal Life (The)	1	8vo	2 50	2
ALEXANDER, A., D.D.				
Moral Science	1	12mo	1 50	3
ALEXANDER, J. W., D.D.				
Alexander, Archibald, Life of, (Portrait)	1	12mo	2 00	3
Christian Faith and Practice (Discourses)	1	12mo	2 00	6
Consolation (Discourses)	1	12mo	2 00	5
Faith (Discourses)	1	12mo	2 00	6
Forty Years' Correspondence with a Friend	2	12mo	4 00	4
Preaching, Thoughts on	1	12mo	2 00	5

	Volumes.	Size.	Price.	Page.
ALEXANDER, J. A., D.D.				
Acts (Commentary)	2	12mo	$4 00	8
Isaiah " (complete)	2	8vo	6 50	7
" " (abridged)	2	12mo	4 00	8
Mark "	1	12mo	2 00	8
Matthew "	1	12mo	2 00	8
Psalms "	3	12mo	6 00	7
New Test. Literature and Ecc. Hist.	1	12mo	2 00	9
Sermons (with Portrait)	2	12mo	——	9
ALLSTON, WASHINGTON.				
Lectures and Poems	1	12mo	2 50	9
ANDREWS, REV. S. J.				
Life of Our Lord	1	post 8vo	3 00	10
ARMSTRONG, G. D., D.D.				
Works of	3	12mo	ea. 1 25	11
BAUTAIN, PROF. A.				
Extempore Speaking	1	12mo	1 50	12
BEECHER, REV. H. W.				
PRAYERS FROM PLYMOUTH PULPIT	1	12mo	1 75	13
BOTTA, PROF.				
Dante as Poet, Patriot, Philosopher	1	crown 8vo	2 50	14
BRACE, CHARLES L.				
Hungary, with Experience of Austrian Police,	1	12mo	——	15
Home Life in Germany	1	12mo	——	14
Norse Folk	1	12mo	2 00	15
Races of Old World	1	post 8vo	2 50	15
Short Sermons for Newsboys	1	16mo	1 50	16
BUSHNELL, HORACE, D.D.				
Character of Jesus	1	18mo	1 00	19
Christ and his Salvation	1	12mo	2 00	19
Christian Nurture	1	12mo	2 00	18
Nature and the Supernatural	1	12mo	2 25	17
New Life, Sermons for	1	12mo	2 00	19
Vicarious Sacrifice, The	1	8vo	3 00	18
Work and Play	1	12mo	2 00	19
CHEEVER, G. B., D.D.				
Works of	3	12mo	——	20
CLARK, PROF. N. G.				
English Language, Elements of	1	12mo	1 25	21
COLLIER, J. PAYNE, F.S.A.				
Rarest Books in English Language	4	small 8vo	12 00	21
CONYBEARE, REV. W. J., and HOWSON, REV. J. S.				
St. Paul, Life and Epistles of (illustrated)	2	8vo	7 50	22

	Volumes.	Size.	Price.	Page.
Cook, Prof. J. P., Jr.				
Religion and Chemistry	1	crown 8vo	$2 50	24
Craik, Geo. L., LL.D.				
English Literature and Language	2	8vo	7 50	23
Crosby, Prof. Howard, D.D.				
New Testament with Notes	1	12mo	1 50	24
Crummell, Rev. A.				
Africa, Future of	1	12mo	1 00	—
Dana, A. H.				
Ethical and Physiological Inquiries	1	12mo	1 50	25
Dana, R. H.				
Poems and Prose Writings	2	12mo	4 00	25
Dawson, Henry B.				
Fœderalist (Univ. Ed.)	1	8vo	3 00	25
" with Notes	1	8vo	3 75	25
Day, Prof. H. N.				
English Composition	1	12mo	1 50	26
Discourse, (Rhetoric)	1	12mo	1 50	26
Logic	1	12mo	1 50	27
Derby, Edward, Earl of.				
Homer's Iliad (translated)	2	crown 8vo	5 00	28
De Vere, M. Schele, LL.D.				
Studies in English	1	crown 8vo	2 50	29
Dingman, J. H.				
Publisher's Sheet-Book	1	Folio	15 00	29
Drummond, Rev. Jas.				
Christian Life, Thoughts for	1	12mo	1 50	30
Duyckinck, E. A. and G. L.				
Cyclopædia of Am. Literature (400 Portraits, &c.)	2	royal 8vo	10 00	31
Dwight, Benj. W.				
Philology, Modern	2	8vo	6 00	30
Ellet, Mrs. E. F.				
American Revolution, Domestic History of	1	12mo	1 50	32
" " Women of	3	12mo	——	33
Pioneer Women of the West	1	12mo	1 50	32
Queens of Am. Society (13 steel engravings)	1	12mo	2 50	33
Elliott, Charles W.				
New England History	2	8vo	6 00	34
Ewbank, Thos.				
Hydraulics	1	8vo	6 00	34
Felter, S. A.				
Arithmetics, Natural Series of	1	——	——	35-36

	Volumes.	Size.	Price.	Page.
FIELD, HENRY M., D.D.				
Atlantic Telegraph, History of . . .	1	12mo	$1 75	37
FISHER, REV. PROF. GEO. P.				
Supernatural Origin of Christianity . .	1	8vo	2 50	38
Silliman, Benj., LL.D., Life of (Portrait)	2	crown 8vo	5 00	37
FORSYTH, WM.				
Cicero, New Life of (Illustrations) . .	2	crown 8vo	5 00	39
FOWLER W. C., LL.D.				
Sectional Controversy (The)	1	8vo	1 75	39
FROUDE, J. A.				
HISTORY OF ENGLAND	10	crown 8vo	3 00 ea.	40
SHORT STUDIES ON GREAT SUBJECTS . .	1	crown 8vo	3 00	41
GAGE, REV. W. L.				
Carl Ritter, Life of	1	12mo	2 00	42
GASPARIN, COUNT.				
America before Europe	1	12mo	2 00	42
GIBBONS, J. S.				
PUBLIC DEBT OF THE UNITED STATES .	1	crown 8vo	2 00	43
GUIZOT, M.				
Meditations (First and Second Series) .	2	12mo ea.	1 75	43
GUYOT, PROF. ARNOLD.				
Geographies, Wall Maps, Key, etc. . . .	–	——	——	44–47
HALL, EDWIN, D.D.				
Puritans and their Principles	1	8vo	2 50	48
HALSEY, REV. LEROY J.				
Bible, Literary Attractions of . . .	1	12mo	1 75	48
HEADLEY, J. T.				
Complete Works of	15			49–53
HEIDELBERG,				
Catechism	1	small 4to	3 50	54
HERBERT, H. W.				
Works of	3	12mo ea.	1 50	54
HOLLAND, DR. J. G. (Timothy Titcomb.)				
Bay-Path. A Novel	1	12mo	2 00	58
Bitter-Sweet. A Poem	1	12mo	1 50	56
Gold Foil	1	12mo	1 75	56
KATHRINA. A Poem	1	12mo	1 50	59
Lessons in Life	1	12mo	1 75	57
Letters to the Joneses	1	12mo	1 75	57
Letters to Young People	1	12mo	1 50	55
Miss Gilbert's Career	1	12mo	2 00	59
Plain Talks on Familiar Subjects . .	1	12mo	1 75	58

	Volumes.	Size.	Price.	Page.
HOURS AT HOME.				
A FAMILY MAGAZINE		Per annum	$3 00	60
HURST, REV. J. F.				
Rationalism, History of	1	8vo	3 50	61
JAMESON, JUDGE J. A.				
Constitutional Convention	1	8vo	4 50	62
JOHNSON, ANNA C. (MINNIE MYRTLE).				
Cottages of the Alps	1	12mo	——	63
Germany, Peasant Life in	1	12mo	——	63
Myrtle Wreath	1	12mo	1 25	63
JONES, CHARLES COLCOCK, D.D.				
HISTORY OF THE CHURCH OF GOD	2	8vo	ea. 3 50	63
KIRKLAND, MRS. C. M.				
Evening Book	1	12mo	1 25	65
Holidays Abroad	2	12mo	2 00	65
Patriotic Eloquence	1	12mo	1 75	64
School Garland	1	12mo	——	64
KNOX, REV. J. B.				
St. Thomas, W. I., History of	1	12mo	$1 25	65
LABOULAYE EDOUARD.				
Paris in America	1	12mo	1 25	69
LANGE, PROF. J. P., D.D.				
Commentary on Scriptures, Theolog. and Homiletical: Matthew (1); MARK AND LUKE (1); ACTS (1); JAMES, PETER, JOHN, JUDE (1); CORINTHIANS (1); THESSALONIANS, TIMOTHY, TITUS, PHILEMON, HEBREWS (1); GENESIS, (1)		8vo	ea. 5 00	66–68
LAWRENCE, EUGENE.				
British Historians, Lives of	2	12mo	3 50	69
LIBER LIBRORUM	1	16mo	1 50	70
LORD, JOHN, LL.D.				
OLD ROMAN WORLD	1	crown 8vo	3 00	70
LYNCH, LIEUT. W. F.				
Naval Life	1	12mo	1 50	71
MCLEOD, ALEX., D.D.				
Life of, by Rev. S. B. Wylie	1	8vo	2 00	114
MACDONALD, J. M., D.D.				
My Father's House	1	12mo	1 50	72
MACLEOD, DONALD,				
Works of	3	12mo	ea. 1 25	71
MAGOON, REV. E. L.				
Living Orators in America	1	12mo	1 75	72
Orators of the American Revolution	1	12mo		72

	Volumes.	Size.	Price.	Page.
MAINE, HENRY S.				
Ancient Law	1	crown 8vo	$3 00	73
MARSH, HON. GEO. P.				
English Language, Lectures on	1	crown 8vo	3 00	74
" " Origin and History of	1	crown 8vo	3 00	74
Man and Nature	1	crown 8vo	3 00	75
MARSH, J., D.D.				
Temperance Recollections	1	12mo	2 25	76
MASON, J. M., D.D.				
Complete Works	4	post 8vo	——	76
MEARS, REV. J. W.				
Bible and the Workshop	1	12mo	1 00	76
MITCHELL, DONALD G. (IK MARVEL).				
Dream Life	1	12mo	$1 75	77
Dr. Johns: A Novel	2	12mo	3 50	79
Fresh Gleanings	1	12mo	——	78
Lorgnette, The	1	12mo	——	78
My Farm of Edgewood	1	12mo	1 75	79
Reveries of a Bachelor	1	12mo	1 75	77
RURAL STUDIES	1	12mo	1 75	80
Seven Stories	1	12mo	1 75	78
Wet Days at Edgewood	1	12mo	1 75	80
MITCHEL, PROF. O. M.				
Astronomy of the Bible	1	12mo	1 75	81
Planetary and Stellar Worlds	1	12mo	1 75	81
Popular Astronomy	1	12mo	1 75	81
MORRIS, GEO. P.				
Poetical Works (blue and gold)	1	16mo	1 50	83
MULLER MAX.				
Science of Language, Lectures on	1	crown 8vo	2 50	82
" " " (Second Series)			3 50	82
NEWCOMB, REV. H.				
Missions, Cyclopædia of (32 Maps)	1	8vo	——	83
ORLEANS, DUCHESS OF.				
Memoirs of (Portrait)	1	12mo		86
OWEN, J. J., D.D.				
Commentaries on the New Testament: *Matthew* (1); MARK AND LUKE (1); JOHN (1); ACTS (—), in press; GENESIS (—), in press	1	12mo ea.	1 75	84–85
PAEZ, DON RAMON.				
South America, Wild Scenes in	1	crown 8vo	2 50	86
PAULDING, JAMES K.				
Literary Life of (1); BULLS AND JONATHANS (1); TALES OF THE GOOD WOMAN (1); A BOOK OF VAGARIES (1); DUTCHMAN'S FIRESIDE . . . each	1	crown 8vo	2 50	87

	Volumes.	Size.	Price.	Page.
PERCE, ELBERT.				
Magnetic Globes			—	88
PERRY, PROF. A. L.				
Political Economy, Elements of	1	crown 8vo	2 50	89
PRENTISS, S. S.				
Life of, by Geo. L. Prentiss, D.D. . .	2	12mo	3 50	86
PRIME, S. I., D.D.				
Power of Prayer	1	12mo	1 50	90
PUBLIC PRAYER.				
Book of	1	12mo	2 00	13
RANDOLPH, A. D. F.				
Hopefully Waiting, and other Verses . .	1	16mo	$1 50	90
SCHAFF, P., D.D.				
Apostolic Church, History of	1	8vo	3 75	91
CHRISTIAN " "	3	8vo ea.	3 75	92–93
PERSON OF CHRIST	1	16mo	1 50	94
SEAMAN, E. C.				
Progress of Nations	1	12mo		94
SHEDD, W. G. T., D.D.				
Christian Doctrine, History of	2	8vo	6 50	95
HOMILETICS AND PASTORAL THEOLOGY .	1	8vo	3 50	96
SHELDON, E. A.				
Model Lessons on Objects, etc.				97
SILLIMAN, BEN. M.D.				
Life of, by Professor Geo. P. Fisher . .	2	crown 8vo	5 00	37
SIMMS, W. G.				
Huguenots in Florida	1	12mo	1 50	—
SMITH, PROF. H. B., D.D.				
Christian Church, History of, in Tabular Form	1	Folio	6 75	98–99
SMITH, J. H.				
Gilead; or, The Vision of All Souls' Hospital	1	12mo	1 50	100
SMITH, MRS. MARY HOWE.				
Lessons on the Globe	1	12mo	0 50	88
SPRING, GARDINER, D.D.				
Personal Reminiscences, etc. (Portrait) .	2	12mo	4 00	100
STANLEY, DEAN A. P.				
Eastern Church	1	8vo	4 00	101
Jewish Church, Lectures on (First Series) .	1	8vo	4 00	101
" " " (Second Series)	1	8vo	5 00	101, 102
Sermons	1	12mo	1 50	103
STRICKLAND, AGNES.				
QUEENS OF ENGLAND, LIVES OF	1	12mo	2 00	103

	Volumes.	Size.	Price.	Page.
TAYLOR, GEORGE.				
Indications of the Creator.	1	12mo	1 75	105
TENNEY, S., A.M.				
Natural History	1	crown 8vo	3 00	104
" " Library Edition	1	large 8vo	4 00	104
" " for Schools	1	12mo	2 00	104
TIMOTHY TITCOMB.				
Complete Works of. See HOLLAND.	—	—	—	55-59
TRENCH, RT. REV. R. C.				
Epistles to Seven Churches, Commentary on	1	12mo	1 50	106
Studies in the Gospels	1	8vo	3 00	106
Glossary of English Words	1	12mo	1 50	107
Synonyms of New Testament (1st and 2d Series)	2	12mo ea.	1 25	107
TUCKERMAN, H. T.				
America and her Commentators	1	crown 8vo	2 50	108
TULLIDGE, REV. H.				
Triumphs of the Bible	1	12mo	2 00	108
TUTHILL, MRS. L. C.				
Joy and Care. Book for Young Mothers	1	16mo	1 00	109
VAN SANTVOORD, GEO.				
Lives of Chief Justices of U. S.	1	8vo		109
WHITNEY, PROF. W. D.				
LANGUAGE, AND THE STUDY OF LANGUAGE	1	crown 8vo	2 50	110
WILLIS, N. P.				
Complete Works of				111, 112
WISE, CAPT. H. A.				
Works of	2	12mo ea.	1 75	112
WOOLSEY, PREST. T. D.				
International Law, Introduction to	1	8vo	2 50	113
WYLIE, S. B., D.D.				
McLeod, Alexander, Life of	1	8vo	2 00	114
ZINCKE, F. BARHAM.				
Extemporary Preaching	1	12mo	1 50	114

ILLUSTRATED GIFT-BOOKS.

*** *In this list the prices of the respective works as bound in cloth, full gilt, are given. All of them, however, are furnished in Turkey morocco, and the prices of these editions may be learned by reference to the catalogue.*

	Price.	Page.		Price.	Page.
ÆSOP'S FABLES	$18 00	117	FRED AND MARIA AND ME	$1 50	121
Bitter-Sweet	9 00	117	*Folk Songs*	15 00	115
Book of Rubies	7 00	119	MY FARM OF EDGEWOOD	10 00	121
Christian Armor	15 00	120	Pilgrim's Progress	5 00	120
Cotter's Saturday Night	5 00	119	QUEENS OF AMERICAN SOCIETY	6 00	118
FLORAL BELLES	25 00	116			

www.ingramcontent.com/pod-product-compliance
Lightning Source LLC
LaVergne TN
LVHW020232110826
845151LV00003B/902

* 9 7 8 1 4 2 5 5 3 0 7 0 9 *